Us v Them

Us v Them

*Journeys to the World's
Greatest Football Derbies*

GILES GOODHEAD

VIKING
an imprint of
PENGUIN BOOKS

VIKING

Published by the Penguin Group
Penguin Books Ltd, 80 Strand, London WC2R 0RL, England
Penguin Putnam Inc., 375 Hudson Street, New York, New York 10014, USA
Penguin Books Australia Ltd, 250 Camberwell Road,
Camberwell, Victoria 3124, Australia
Penguin Books Canada Ltd, 10 Alcorn Avenue, Toronto, Ontario, Canada M4V 3B2
Penguin Books India (P) Ltd, 11 Community Centre,
Panchsheel Park, New Delhi – 110 017, India
Penguin Books (NZ) Ltd, Cnr Rosedale and Airborne Roads,
Albany, Auckland, New Zealand
Penguin Books (South Africa) (Pty) Ltd, 24 Sturdee Avenue,
Rosebank 2196, South Africa

Penguin Books Ltd, Registered Offices: 80 Strand, London WC2R 0RL, England

www.penguin.com

First published 2003
1

Set in 12/14.75pt Monotype Bembo
Typeset by Rowland Phototypesetting Ltd, Bury St Edmunds, Suffolk
Printed in Great Britain by Clays Ltd, St Ives plc

A CIP catalogue record for this book is available from the British Library

ISBN 0-670-91340-5

Dedicated to:
Walter James Shaw (Woolwich Arsenal)
James Warner (Aston Villa)

Fixture List

Acknowledgements

I'd like to thank the following generous people for advice, encouragement, belief or tickets: Sheila Atkinson, Simon Baker, Matthew Batstone, Florie Brizel, Marshall Cooper, Wayne Cooper, Mark Fuller, Jorgé Galiano, Jane and Neil Goodhead, Nancy Hammerman, Gabor Komarony, Tony Lacey, Peter Loewenberg, Gary Martin, Peter Nalle, Fernando Parfumi, Esther Perry, Richard Savage, Paul and Harold Ure and Alan Webber. And last, but really first, Claire Perry.

Special thanks to fellow travellers Brett, Toby, Nigel, Gene and Jo-an, Grafton, Neil, and David.

Introduction

Imagine this: you're in the top deck at Barcelona, one atom among a hundred thousand faces. It's 8.55 on a sultry evening. Far below and out of sight the teams are clattering through the tunnel, studs on concrete, faces tight, flashbulbs popping. The year is 1960. General Franco rules Spain from Madrid and here in Barcelona you can't vote and your Catalan flag is outlawed. Suddenly the Real Madrid team runs out to the brilliant green field – Puskas, Di Stefano – Real are European champions yet again, but they're met by a cacophony of booing. On comes the home team and the whistles turn to a belly-roar of defiance. The flag may be banned but there it is anyway, on eleven Barcelona shirts lining up for battle. The crowd chants 'Visca el Barça!' over and over. The ball waits on the centre spot for the referee's whistle. Drums pound. Winning this football game tonight is beyond desire, it's the only thing that matters.

This is a book with a few angles. Most obviously it's a book about really good football: some of the greatest enduring rivalries between local clubs. Eight games I have always wanted to experience before I get too middle-aged, lethargic, and fixated on growing potatoes. A what-the-heck pilgrimage to legendary stadiums packed to the rafters with flags and klaxons, flares and smoke: the Nou Camp, the San Siro, the Azteca . . .

Then again, it's not really about football at all. These are games where the neighbourhood rivalry goes far beyond ninety minutes huffing and puffing. Franco is long dead but Barça still take on Madrid year after year to assert their Catalonian identity. Glasgow's Old Firm is a religious schism around the Irish Question. In Buenos Aires' Superclásico, the Millonarios of posh River Plate fend off Boca Juniors, Maradona's old *barrio* boys.

Clan warfare, simply put. The trouble with wars is that they're scary, and football does have its fear-factor. The first match I ever went to (not counting Billericay Town versus Ed Stewpot's Top Ten Eleven, where the referee scored for the pop stars and reduced me to tears) was Bolton Wanderers up against Chelsea in West London. Scurrying through a cordon of police on horses with plexiglas shields over their big wild eyes, I remember being petrified. Nothing was happening, but fear was in football's bones.

These days I live in Los Angeles, the real theatre of dreams. This is the town where a pony-tailed Buddhist ballooned his penalty to lose one World Cup final while a woman called Brandi nailed hers to win another, and the only thing most locals remember about either game was the woman ecstatically ripping off her shirt. Admittedly, both matches were goalless draws.

One evening a friend took me to see the Los Angeles Lakers play basketball. They're called the Lakers because of all the lakes two thousand miles away in Minnesota, where the team once played. After drinks in a brassy bar at the Staples Center, we found our seats just beneath tiers of corporate boxes draped with gorgeous yawning women. A peppy waitress beamed in our orders for over-stuffed carvery sandwiches. Below us, the Laker Girls gyrated to deafening rap music. Both teams ran hard, in bursts between television breaks. Jack Nicholson sat court-side, but Pamela Anderson got the lustiest cheer, bouncing out of her seat to wave on the jumbo screens. It was warm and comfortable, with plenty of impressive dunks from Shaquille O'Neal and the other seven-foot-tall actors in Nikes. The closest we got to any dissent was when a call went against Shaq and a few people booed, but jovially. All in all, a pleasant, pricey evening's entertainment, made for TV in corporate America. Nobody chanted 'You're going home in a fuckin' ambulance' and nobody threw coins with sharpened edges. Not a whiff of danger but, perhaps, an absence of meaning.

That's why encounters like Barça against Madrid or Rangers against Celtic are special. Sit at Ibrox on a gloomy Glasgow afternoon and you sense in your gut that there's a larger issue being played out as the tackles fly in. Nobody leaves a good derby match as a neutral spectator. How do you feel when Rangers fans start up with their song about the imprisoned IRA man who died on hunger strike? 'Could you go a chicken supper, Bobby Sands?' Picking sides means taking a stance.

I decided I wanted to taste these confrontations, in the cities where they still matter, even if it wasn't entirely safe. After all, you can't expect genuine intensity without genuine antagonism. You can't have it both ways. I wanted to see what was left of the origins of football, those medieval battles where my village's youths would try to stuff a pig's bladder into your village's well, resulting in a three-day brawl. I wanted to experience raw soccer on derby day.

And like Goldilocks, what I discovered seemed just right. The games were feisty, but rarely boiled over into hooliganism, and then just dumbell-heads clouting each other on easily avoided street corners. Barcelona and Tottenham's fans were entertainingly full of bile after losing star players to the enemy. In Istanbul, six thousand cops glared through their visors at thirty thousand demented Turks. Even among Milan's fashionistas and Prague's intellectuals, their cross-town rivalries still registered as grudge games. Only in Buenos Aires was the blood pressure so high that the Argentinian government was on the verge of cancelling football entirely.

But enough pre-match analysis. Time to scrounge some tickets and get on a plane.

A Note about the Games

Why Istanbul, but not Rio? Why nothing in Asia? Why Spurs versus Arsenal instead of Everton versus Liverpool? Come on, ref!

Any selection of football derbies is bound to have controversial decisions. I can only apologize to anyone left fuming at my picks. If you see bias, you're probably right. These are simply eight games that caught my fancy. Arguments about which are really the 'greatest' local rivalries are best tackled over a few beers in your favourite pub. My final choice of destinations was skewed by things like air miles, open weekends and luck getting tickets.

I will say that I enjoyed the journey – really, a breathless series of long weekends – tremendously. I was lucky too: twenty-seven goals (3.4 per game), three red cards, five penalties (four in one game), passionate full-houses and not much trouble. There is nothing like a game of football for uniting the world and simultaneously dividing it into tribes. And there's nothing sweeter than dancing behind the goal on the night your team wins the derby.

Giles Goodhead

Cabrón

Start big, as they say in musicals, and what's bigger than Barcelona versus Real Madrid? I reckoned picking Spain's biggest football rivalry for my first taste of derby fervour wouldn't be hard to arrange. All I needed was a plane, a bed and, of course, a ticket to the game. Since Barça's stadium is massive, even the match ticket shouldn't be a problem. But a quick check of FC Barcelona's official website suggested otherwise. They had over 100,000 paid-up members. There were no tickets for anyone else, apart from a handful at the stadium a few days before each match, which presumably would go to the kind of fanatics who had slept on the pavement for the previous week. It would have to be the secondary market then.

I live in Los Angeles. Local ticket agencies were vague about Barcelona and Madrid as places, let alone as a glittering sporting event, so I started calling London. 'Nah problem, guvnuh,' 'Arry of Front Row Tickets told me, 'I can get you in. Leave it to me, mate.'

Next I called the airlines and asked for a cheap flight the following week. The helpful lady at Iberia explained patiently that cheap fares were 'only for the advertising', and that there weren't really any such rates available – 'Well, maybe one ticket, but not any more, you know.' I told her it didn't seem a terribly effective form of advertising and asked her what I should do. Muffled clacking on her keyboard. A long pause. 'Can you go next year?'

Of course I couldn't. I had to go NOW. Real Madrid was probably the biggest team in Europe. Barça's Nou Camp was the biggest stadium in Europe. Both teams had squads made up completely of international all-stars: at the time, Rivaldo and Roberto Carlos of Brazil, Raúl and Luis Enrique of Spain, Marc Overmars and Patrick Kluivert of Holland. Arguably the season's biggest star, the Portuguese Luis Figo, had just quit Barça in murky circumstances, for none other than arch-rival Madrid, and for a fee that made him the world's most expensive footballer. Word was that Barça fans – Catalonians who maintain a healthy animosity to Madrid that goes back well before the invention of football – were preparing a specially vitriolic welcome for their former idol. Two hundred thousand whistles were going to be handed out to the fans at the stadium. Why they needed two each, I couldn't figure.

If flights were elusive, hotels were hopeless. To my horror, Barcelona was full, thanks to a bunch of trade shows, the match itself, and Europe's ongoing love affair with the city as a weekend fling. The Internet search engines scanned their databases and came back with dirt-cheap rooms in Andorra, a skiing destination a few hundred kilometres to the north and, yes, technically another country. Should have planned ahead, tut-tutted an irritating inner voice. Last Minute Travel (dot.com) looked hopeful for a moment, but then advised me to go instead to New Orleans. Finally, goggle-eyed and room-less after a solid morning pointing and clicking, I quit my web-browser and went for a frustrated stroll along Hollywood Boulevard's Walk of Fame, where hundreds of lame-looking tourists shuffled aimlessly past lame T-shirt shops, pointing their cameras at lame dead stars embedded in the baking hot pavement.

The day before I was supposed to leave, things looked grim. I had a pricey plane reservation but there was *nada* on the hotel front, although my brother-in-law was networking at Sony Music and thought 'something might turn up'. I wasn't happy about the prospect of kipping in the train station, but that was a minor problem compared with my missing match ticket.

When I'd called 'Arry back to make sure he had my ticket, he continued in his friendly, optimistic, no hassles vein, but then asked me to give him the time, date and place again, which suggested that he hadn't done anything yet. 'Call tomorrow,' he said. When I did, someone told me that 'Arry was gone for the rest of the week. Suddenly I was in Monty Python's cheese shop, trying to buy a nice piece of Stilton and getting the runaround.

'So give me your address, then,' said 'Arry's back-up Alfie.

'It's too late now,' I whined. 'By the time it gets here I'll be there.'

'We'll send it back to Viva España then,' suggested Alfie.

'But I don't have an address you can send it to.'

'Blimey,' said Alfie, 'ever 'eard of shit creek, 'ave you?'

My wife offered tea and sympathy. 'You know, getting there's half the fun.'

I took a sip. 'I always wondered why people said that.'

But my petty logistical problems were nothing compared with the mess Figo was in. Asked for his thoughts about the upcoming game at a Madrid press conference, he responded that fans pay their money and are entitled to cheer, or for that matter, whistle whoever they want. He hoped that things would not become 'excessive'. The pack of journos wanted more. Was he now loyal to Madrid, they teased? '¿*Madridista*? *Yo soy portugués*.' Nobody in Barcelona was buying this line. Just the kind of thing a traitor, a turncoat, a Judas would say. I could imagine truckloads of whistles lumbering towards the stadium.

Of course, being a foreigner wasn't helping Figo's case. Top-flight European clubs have lost their local roots. Years ago, Liverpool used to win with British players, Bayern with Germans and Ajax with Dutch. Not any more. National borders are disappearing across Europe and nowhere is this more visible than in football. The continent's top ten teams, the ones with the biggest TV deals and the most money, now hunt for the best twenty players they can induce to quit somewhere else, regardless of nationality. Sometimes these teams play with no locals at all, and everyone knows that player loyalty is becoming quaint and rustic – secondary to winning, anyway. Barcelona would potentially start with five Dutch against Madrid – Barçajax, some local wags called them, not altogether kindly. Figo was just another mercenary, good enough to play for any team, good enough to represent a fantasy capture for Real. And, it seemed, bribable.

Florentino Pérez, a Madrid-based tycoon, decided that he wanted to get elected as President of Real Madrid, a position roughly as important as that of Spanish Prime Minister. Campaigning on the manifesto that if he was elected Luis Figo would come to Real, Pérez won. Figo was next seen at a press conference sheepishly holding up a white number ten shirt. Barcelona got a buy-out fee of ten billion pesetas, or about sixty million euros, the going rate for a creative midfield genius with superb crossing ability from either flank and a pile-driver shot. Plenty of money to buy a new batch of replacement stars, but the Loss of Figo felt like the Fall of Barcelona itself, back in September 1714, when Catalonia finally lost its independence from Madrid following almost a century of peasant rebellion.

Then it emerged that Figo had signed a side deal with Pérez, guaranteeing him a large payment just for promising to come to Madrid, payable even if Pérez lost. Hence the image in a Catalonian newspaper showing a grimacing Figo-face on a ten billion peseta banknote, under the headline 'Figo Pesetero'. Hence the sixteen-page special section on La Traición, 'The Betrayal'.

Hours before setting off I got good news on the lodging front. My brother-in-law had spoken to a colleague who had a drinking acquaintance who had a relative, etc. etc. Allegedly someone called Natalie had an apartment in Barcelona but did not need it this weekend. All I had to do was call her mobile. Reaching her in a noisy restaurant on the seventh try, she agreed that yes, for a modest consideration, she was prepared to let a complete stranger have the run of her house. She sounded sceptical, as if perhaps her boss had asked her to do it. It was 'too complicated' to give me the address now, she said, but suggested we meet when I arrived in Barcelona. Hanging up, I felt doubtful that this vague arrangement could possibly work, but I left Los Angeles with an incriminating-looking Post-it note with Natalie's name and number.

As for the match ticket, I resorted to making a one-night reservation in a pricey hotel – the only space I'd found in days of fruitless searching – simply to have an address where the ticket could be expressed, and in case Natalie changed her mind and turned off her cellphone. Passport and a few million pesetas in my pocket, I was cleared for take-off.

I asked the flight attendant for a glass of port in honour of poor

Luis Figo, as I'd started thinking of him, facing a hundred thousand people armed with whistles, and each with a second whistle as back-up in their pockets! I also figured that a strong, sweet drink might sufficiently anaesthetize me to induce sleep. The attendant searched his cart and came up with a Californian red wine. 'It's kinda like port,' he said, in that blank way Americans have when dealing with wacky foreign requests.

This amused the man sharing my personal space for the night, who turned out to be Dutch and decisive. He said he'd lived in Barcelona for years. He was returning home from an advertising convention in New Orleans, and was working through a cluster of miniatures of Scotch. He planned to watch the game on TV.

'Cheaper,' he said. 'And I'm not so interested.'

'How do you like living there?' I asked him.

'Best place. In the world.'

'Why?'

'Food, climate, civilized, beach, mountains, history, convenient location, the women. You want more?'

'Sounds like California,' I said. 'Maybe apart from the history.'

'You crazy? That's not civilized. Look at those people.'

He had a point. 'So maybe I should move my family to Barcelona,' I said.

'Christ, no.' He knocked back another Johnny Walker.

'But why not, if it's so great?'

'The schools. Language problem. You want your kids to grow up speaking Catalan? That's what they teach. Civic pride. What use is a crazy mixed-up tongue like Catalan? No use. Like Afrikaans. Useless. Isolated. Dumb.' Abruptly he fell asleep.

As we flew east through the night I drowsed fitfully. With my fake hotel reservation and rendezvous with the mysterious Natalie, one small bag and a passport, I felt like an anonymous mole out of Le Carré. Travelling to a distant city where I'd know no one, to witness a footballing assassination, alone and barely able to speak – it was a little scary, like the first day of term in a strange classroom.

I went to an old-fashioned English public school, where fear and footer were the dominant flavours of my teenage years. I was afraid of a sadistic gym teacher who communicated only through a series of coded whistles and brandished a plastic baseball bat known as 'the yellow peril'. I was afraid of tough kids from town who would grab our ornate peaked caps and hurl them over walls. I was even afraid of the giggling conspiratorial girls from the nearby convent school who sat upstairs on the bus to smoke fags and snog the more delinquent boys who seemed – incredibly – to find this fun.

The School Song celebrated our founding in 1557 when they burned a boy at the stake by an old red wall. I don't recall why they burned him, but it seemed an appropriate way to launch such an educational establishment. Continuing the tradition, more recently a boy had jumped to his death from an upstairs window – drugs, went the whisper – while another belly-flopped into the swimming pool and, allegedly, had burst open. On the plus side we were national champions at fencing.

Our school motto was 'virtue, learning and manners'. To encourage virtue, we were shown colour slides of penises with dramatic outbreaks of herpes. As for learning, the biology master had us dissect a stunned locust using only a pin, while 'Gut', our headmaster, taught elocution and Latin by holding the spike of a drawing compass at the back of your neck to help you recall, say, the third person plural pluperfect conjugation of *capio*. Failures of manners were typically punished via canings, beatings or running laps of 'drill' around the school's grounds until you threw up.

Every Friday afternoon the entire school dressed in khaki uniforms and was frogmarched around the quadrangle by masters with genuine army credentials. Obviously, the combination of our fencing, marching and politeness prowess would be terrifically useful should there ever be a recurrence of the English Civil War. To further instil manliness, swimming was compulsory in the frigid outdoor pool, whether you could swim or not. I remember one crisp morning jumping in (two short whistles) and then being made to clamber out (three long) and line up over and over again, shivering miserably in the chill breeze.

The saving grace was football. I was – we all were – football crazy. In keeping with the school ethos of mass participation regardless of ability or interest, every boy was assigned to some level of football team, which played twice a week through mud, rain, gale or hail. The truly feeble had only two ways to escape, either volunteer to referee or endure elocution with Gut and his metal spikes.

My own footballing career was a slow decline from a starring role on the wing for the under elevens to make-weight and finally bench-warmer. At whatever level, the games were treated as astoundingly vital, as if the future of the British Empire depended on the outcome. One gusty afternoon I was promoted to my house first team thanks to a serious flu epidemic. We lost the game against East House 2–0, while our housemaster 'HB' raved along the sideline. 'Get forward!' 'Shoot!' 'No, no, no, no, NO!' I was anonymous, lots of huffing where the ball had just been, until one critical moment when a ricochet spun my way and I was through with a shot on the East House goal. Rather than just smack the ball in I tried a cheeky chip over their sprawling keeper. The ball floated through the air, plonked impossibly on the top of the crossbar and bounced away.

I couldn't believe it. 'What do we have to DO to score?' ranted HB, tearing at his grey hair, while I burned with shame at my gaping miss. It was so utterly important to him, and therefore to me, that his claret shirts beat East. I imagined the poor man, an ageing bachelor, sitting in his ratty school flat that evening with a pot of stewed tea and cigarettes, going over the traumatic near-misses of the afternoon in something approaching despair.

Barcelona was dark and murky. We climbed down to one of those oversized buses and lurched past rows of parked planes towards the distant terminal. As we walked along the passages to Customs, I overheard my neighbour from the flight telling someone else about me. It was in Dutch, but the gist was clear: this crazy guy came six thousand miles just for a football match! I'd half expected to see other fans at the airport, maybe a few wearing Barça's famous red and blue, or possibly some visiting Madrid fans and lines of riot police ready to leap in and wave batons. But there was no sign that there even was a game the next day. Waving my passport, I had my first inkling of doubt that perhaps it was all hype. Maybe the historic animosity was just that, a relic. Maybe Catalonia no longer defined itself by antagonism to Madrid. Maybe this was a football match, nothing more.

At the giant Plaça de Catalunya, Barcelona was busy going to work. It was overcast, cool, leaves were blowing around skittishly and I felt in dire need of a comfortable bed, which reminded me to check on my sleeping arrangements. So I tried calling Natalie, expecting that this would be the first of twenty or so increasingly desperate calls through the day. Instead she answered with a snappy 'Hola'. I was in no state to attempt Spanish, let alone Catalan.

'I have arrived,' I said, somewhat grandly. 'I am in the big square in the middle.'

'Aah, already?' she said.

'Yes. I came on the train. I am here in Barcelona. Now.' This seemed pretty clear.

'I have no milk,' she said, taking me by surprise. Was this her excuse to withdraw her apartment? 'So I must go out for coffee. I will see you at ten, okay?'

My *Time Out* map suggested that I could walk to her street, saving the palaver of figuring out taxi etiquette and then arriving with an hour to sit on her doorstep, arousing the local gossips. I set off, my suitcase on wheels humming obediently behind. In the pointlessly comparative manner of a newly arrived tourist I decided that Barcelona was like Paris: wide boulevards, quiet side streets and an amazing frequency of cafés and restaurants. Less dog mess, perhaps. The intersections were built as octagons, which gave the traffic more space to turn, but forced me to veer all over the place when crossing each street. And with similarly spacey thoughts I ambled to Natalie's flat, arriving on the dot of ten, just a minute ahead of her.

She offered to carry my case upstairs, apologizing all the way for the lack of a lift, the tricky door key ('he is very naughty'), the dark stairwell, the five flights up, the cloudy weather, her English, the small size of her flat, and Spain's historic stance of refusing to extradite suspected criminals to England. Well, not the last one.

Actually, I liked the flat immediately. Everything was compact and efficient, like the two-burner stove next to the washer-dryer in the corner of her main room. Through the window was a clutter of rooftops with washing lines and satellite dishes. I thanked her very much for helping me out and asked where she was going for the weekend? She said that she would stay with her boyfriend, but she had recently found this flat and was going to move into it soon. This sounded like a potentially troubled conversation so I changed the subject. Where did she recommend I eat? There was a wonderful place right downstairs with a menu full of local specialities. Was she going to watch the game, I wondered? Oh no, she wasn't interested. And her boyfriend had been very 'hilarious' – was that the word? – to hear how far I had travelled just for a game of football.

After she left, I took a shower in a stall about the size of a fat man's coffin. You could stand inside with your arms folded, but any attempt to wave them around – applying shampoo for example – was impossible. The water was on a knife-edge between icy and scalding in the time-honoured European manner, so I emerged a little less sold on compact city penthouses and set off on the most vital step of my mission – tracking down my ticket to the match.

I bought the day's *Mundo Deportivo* and picked a busy coffee shop where the waiters proceeded to serve everyone except me, despite my raised eyebrows every time one hurried past. 'Twenty-four hours of Barça–Madrid!' shouted the front page, along with a score-line of 3–1, which momentarily horrified me – had I missed it? – until I realized that these were only the goals scored by Barça's Rivaldo and Real's Figo in Champion's League matches earlier in the week. I struggled through twenty pages on 'el superderby', all obsessing on the man they once adored but now had to hate. How was he finding life in Madrid? 'He is far from the ocean, even with his flaming red Porsche Carrera.' What was Barça's coach saying about the traitor? 'The rival of tomorrow is Real Madrid, not Señor Figo.' And just how hot was the swine's Swiss model girlfriend? Look at this cheesecake shot of her frolicking in a skimpy black bikini. Best of all was Figo Pesetero, the mock banknote now upgraded to a cut-out-and-brandish poster.

Still coffee-less I found the hotel where Alfie had promised to remind 'Arry to express my ticket. I began a rambling explanation of having a reservation but not wanting it, and cancelling it if possible, even though it was under twenty-four hours' notice but hoping nevertheless they had a packet for me that had tickets . . . Wordlessly the desk manager produced said packet. Inside was a ticket. It looked genuine. It had tomorrow's date, but oddly, no time. I asked the manager if he knew. Oddly, he didn't. 'I'm not interested in football,' he claimed, something I was rapidly tiring of hearing since it didn't fit with my visions of delirious soccer-mad throngs.

But the locals' lack of interest didn't matter – all elements of my master-plan were now in place. Ticket tucked safely away, I went in search of Barcelona's craziest building (there are many contenders), a half-complete towering fantasy that looks like a gigantic Gothic cathedral that has melted and then been electrocuted. The eccentric architect Gaudí spent forty years working on the Sagrada Familia, often sleeping on the construction site. It's a perfect identity for the city: ambitious, under construction, stylish, impractical, dramatic, unique, absurd.

You could say exactly the same thing about the city's football club too. Most teams are thrilled to bits when they eke out a result, but for a handful of big glamour clubs like Barça or Manchester United, there's a romantic notion that they'd rather lose dramatically than win ugly. Say you're a goal up with ten minutes to play. The smart tactic is to pull men back, soak up the pressure, work the clock. But defence is boring. Toreadors don't keep running away from the bull until night falls. They preen and prance, then go for the jugular. Why dribble to the corner flag when you can sweep upfield for one more swirling attack? Why erect a quick obvious church when you can spend a century on a massive folly? I admired it for forty minutes and then took off for lunch.

Barcelona has lunch nailed. You have to wait until at least two, but then thousands of small neighbourhood places serve up a *menú del día* which offers appetizer, main dish, dessert and wine for about five euros. I quickly fell in love with *all i oli*, which is garlic with olive oil and an egg yolk, dolloped aggressively over salad. The gorgonzola smeared liberally over my chewy *biftek* was equally hostile. As for the *vino tinto*, I'd been expecting a glass, but you get a whole bottle. It was rough but guzzleable. As jetlag washed over me I happily watched the other diners, some reading the Figo papers, a good sign that the entire match wasn't being played just for my benefit. A bunch of businessmen were getting drunk and an elderly couple surreptitiously slipped most of their food to a small dog badly hidden under the table, not that the waitress appeared to care. Following my guidebook's advice on acting like a local, I left a miserly tip. A nap was tempting, but I felt an obligation to behave like a proper tourist and hit a few more cultural highlights.

I bought a red Barça cap and wore it with a gnawing worry that I seemed to be the only person doing so. After a confused walk through the Barri Gòtic, I found the excellent Picasso museum. His early stuff is effortless and wide-eyed, like watching teenage Pelé win the 1958 World Cup. Then I tore up the hill to Miró's place. Miró is fine, especially on coffee mugs, but easily the best thing there was a small sculpture entitled *Chocolate Profiterole* by Claes Oldenburg, boxed in a corner of the random contributions room. It was obviously created by Claes in a fit of pissiness and looked exactly like a plastic replica dog turd available in any good novelty shop.

I trace my love of rebellious art to Colonel Roddy. He ran my school's art department along with Colonel Featherstone. Just as you'd expect from two Second World War British army officers, they taught painting with precision. Bald, gaunt Colonel Roddy dispensed paint in plastic eggcups, four per boy. On no account could you muddy the colours. The colonel violently punched the wall to emphasize the point and his Salvador Dali moustache bounced up and down from the impact. Here was the Roddy School method for painting sky: lay a white wash across the top half of your paper. Then add a thin red line just above the horizon, a yellow line one inch higher, a green one an inch above that and blue on top. No talking at the back. Then rinse your brush, take more white and blend in your four lines with big lateral strokes. Sky inspection in five minutes.

Needless to say, we acted up. Knotted art aprons make great weapons. But Colonel Roddy didn't tolerate rowdiness. 'Quiet, all of you! Brushes down. Stand up. Straight! Cowley and Pepper, see me after. Stand on your chairs, the lot of you. Stand on your desks! Fingers on lips! Five minutes silence!'

I actually came top in art, that first term. My skies were textbook. But when Colonel Roddy went away on manoeuvres, I made a jazzy, freewheeling abstract. I used black, which the colonel insisted was not a colour. I came bottom and felt a warm glow of resentment, like a proper, misunderstood artist.

By now it was late afternoon and I decided that I had lost the plot a little. Barça *ultras* don't hang out in art galleries. It was time for some street-level living. Time for sex.

After handing over my money I walked hesitatingly up a steep staircase painted glossy red. In the entry hall stood a six-foot sculptured penis. And this, I'm afraid, was as good as it got at the Museum of Erotica. A five minute tour revealed a few dozen old framed *Playboy* covers, dodgy black and white snaps of old Barcelona vaudeville houses when the ladies were roly-poly, some seen-it-before pages from the Kama Sutra, and a few hundred more cocks from around the world, mostly small, in glass boxes just like Oldenburg's excrement. And cock sculpture is a limited niche: there's only so much you can do with the basic concept, just as there are only so many ways of fitting human bodies together, genitally speaking. The mere mechanics of sex, dumped into exhibition cases and labelled by a dullard, were remarkably mundane, not erotic at all. ('Balinese penis gong: nineteenth century. Gong made of local wood and used as musical instrument with penis as stick. Artist unknown.')

Although as a punter I knew I'd just been ripped off, I suspected that there was probably a nice little earner lurking up the red stairs. Anyone could come up with a comparable permanent collection by visiting a news-stand and a few antique bookstores. I stopped for a *bichera* – it's a coffee – to think over the figures. Let's say an annual 'art' budget of a thousand pounds, tops, including some cheap plastic frames. Rent could run to another grand a month. Then you've got two part-time ticket takers at minimum wage, let's be generous and say ten pounds an hour. All in, you're looking at well under forty thousand quid per year. On the revenue side, admission is just a fiver (about right, given the pathetic nature of the pleasures within). My guess was they managed twenty suckers an hour which, multiplied by ten hours a day, gives you an annual gross of a quarter of a million. Deduct your costs and you're left with over two hundred thou in pure profit and you get to be a patron of the arts and live in Barcelona where you needn't ever go into your own crummy 'museum'.

Feeling hungry again, I nipped back to my miniature apartment to pick up a coat for dinner. There I was diverted by a rabble-rousing TV programme which involved motor-mouth pundits talking (in Catalan) about The Figo Situation. It was fascinating. They showed Real Madrid's team bus driving from airport to hotel (clearly identified, in case you felt like going down there to blow whistles all night). Kids on scooters swerved around the bus like angry mosquitoes. Then they showed a telling clip from a few years ago when the Danish player Laudrup also moved from Barcelona to Madrid. At the next encounter, Laudrup was jeered from start to final whistle. At one point the ball rolls out of play and Laudrup trots over to take the throw. A Barça trainer stands a couple of yards away with the ball at his feet. Laudrup waits to be given the ball. The trainer ignores him, refuses to recognize that the player exists any more, before finally flicking the ball to a different Madrid player further away, like slapping a cheek with a leather glove.

The programme then launched into a medley of every goal that Barça has ever scored against Real Madrid since television cameras were invented. This had an uplifting effect, like being in a crowd watching a politician you despise receive a near-endless flogging. After the goal-fest, the programme closed by promoting a website called antifigo.com, where an animated Figo dropped his trousers upon your click. It was apparently receiving so many hits that if it had been the real Figo upping and downing his shorts, he'd be far too tired to play tomorrow, which would be a shame since the Ordeal of the Traitor was obviously the focal point of the entire affair.

Finally I settled down with my guidebook to choose a restaurant. My criteria were straightforward, but perhaps ambitious. I required somewhere:

a) serving authentic Catalonian fare
b) classy enough to provide a memorable dining experience, yet not so classy that dining alone would take for ever with no one else to talk to
c) located in a fun part of town
d) with a lively, convivial atmosphere
e) with Barça die-hards gearing up for the big match

My research took a good hour before I had a handful of folded-down pages, so it was well past ten when I set off. This solved the problem of arriving too early for dinner and being the only customer in a silent room. Ignoring the restaurant downstairs that Natalie had recommended – too easy – my first call was a tapas bar in a nearby leafy square. I eased into the last remaining table and began my usual ritual of being ignored by speeding waiters. The place was buzzing but it seemed a yuppie crowd, more people who weren't going to bother watching the game. So after some spicy calamares and a swift beer, I moved on to my main hope, a highly recommended temple of gastronomy a few streets away.

I never like walking into a dining room without spying on it first, in case it's empty or full of nuns. This restaurant had windows set high in the wall so I was only able to conduct reconnaissance by making little jumps as I strolled past discreetly. After making a second pass, I realized that I probably appeared to the elderly patrons inside like an idiot on a pogo stick. In truth the place looked too rarified, somewhere where waiters would scurry over to straighten your napkin if you so much as burped. Surprisingly, they were due to close in forty minutes, so I could see myself keeping a small squadron of staff hanging around while I worked through a seven-course spectacular. No Barça fans there either, so I moved on to my back-ups, by now dizzy with hunger.

In a passage off one of the glitzy shopping boulevards two rival eateries faced each other and each was hopping. I dithered for a while, rating the crowds swarming around each brassy doorway. One seemed just too hip, so I picked the other and pushed inside, holding up one finger to the roving maître d'. He shook his head and strode off. Back on the street, I peered through the smoked window of the too-hip place, gauging how long the wait for a table would be. Judging from the throng around the bar, we were back in 'can you come next year?' territory. I trudged off, realizing that I'd come down with EPD – excessively picky disease.

It was now well after eleven. Momentarily considering retreat to the hole in the wall right below my apartment, I decided instead to tough things out. So I headed for the Ramblas, Barcelona's great walking street packed with cafés, clubs, news kiosks, tourists, spray-painted people who pretend to be human statues and even – allegedly – Barça fans. I'd been saving it for tomorrow night after the game.

No luck. I marched along rejecting dozens of places: too loud, too full, too ice-cream parlourish, too Burger King, too empty, too pricey, too Italian – what was the point of going to Catalonia and then eating spaghetti? In a thoroughly bad mood I kept on walking, around midnight reaching Port Olímpic. It was dead and deserted, like a fish market in the evening. I was famished and at the end of my tether when I came across a couple of restaurants right on the beach. My guidebook described one of them as having the sexiest waitresses in town with wild acts on stage, and although this wasn't much of an endorsement of the cuisine, I had to admit it piqued my fancy. Sadly the reality was more like a slow Wednesday at the Best Western bargain buffet and disco on the edge of Des Moines, Iowa (I've been). They were playing Billy Idol under a revolving mirrored ball and although the *señoritas* were indeed cute, I had come too far to end up in such a dump. It was twelve-thirty in the morning, time to put an end to this farce. With no more hesitation I turned next door and went into what was, as far as I was concerned, the last restaurant in Barcelona. Two minutes later I was sitting with a glass of *tinto*, shoes off below the table, basking under a heat-lamp, with the sound of waves spilling on sand nearby in the dark. I ordered asparagus, spicy potatoes, and something mysterious that involved beef and a chocolate tart.

Who knows why Figo went? Perhaps it was a straightforward wish for more pesetas. Maybe he didn't like his team-mates. Or it just felt like time for a fresh start. When I left London for California I certainly didn't have any great reasons. George Best went there when the wheels came off his footballing career. Me and George Best, then, except I didn't have his highlight reel. I'd wanted to be a footballer – a left winger, specifically – far more deeply than most boys, relentlessly hitting a ball against the garage door evening after evening, trying diving headers into heaps of leaves, feinting past the apple trees in our garden, ball at my toes. My great great uncle James Warner played in goal for Aston Villa and he won the FA Cup in 1887 – 2–0 over West Brom – wearing impossibly long breeches. But as my own role on football teams grew first marginal and then occasional, I realized with deep gloom that I was as inept at banana free kicks and splitting an offside trap as I was smart about Keynesian fiscal policy and the rise of Abstract Expressionist painting.

I passed my exams. I went to university. I graduated. I got a job in London. Strategic planning. But as I walked along the Cromwell Road with my weekly bag of groceries from Sainsbury's, I didn't feel particularly in charge of who I was. I felt bland. My likely path seemed stodgy and conformist: buy a flat, settle down, move to a comfortable burb. In many ways it was the definition of victory but I knew I'd already failed on my own terms, absurd though they were. The future was a wimpy, fur-lined rut, the shortest and dullest route from here to the Colonel Roddy sunset. So I quit my job and emigrated to the land of cults and money obsession, becoming my own *pesetero*. Me and Luis Figo.

Abandoning ship was fun. Closing my bank account, buying a

one-way flight, my uncle in San Diego just off his nuclear submarine writing to say he'd found me an Oldsmobile – I thought this was slang and wrote back to say that actually I wanted a *new* car. Stoic silence from my family and a sneer from an argumentative old sod in a pub who said, 'Why would anyone want to go to California? It's all sun and traffic jams.' As opposed to freezing fog and the M25, I suppose. I couldn't explain it to him, but America was the new place where no one would know who I really was, the boy who'd missed a sitter against East House. In America I imagined I would get the privilege of supervising my own fresh start.

Full and content, I caught a Metro just before two in the morning and walked through quiet side streets to my apartment. As I wiggled the naughty key in its unyielding lock, the local hole in the wall was still packed to the gills, wooden benches groaning with food, genuine-looking locals toasting each other, singing drunkenly. There was even someone – at last – wearing a Barça shirt!

I'd spent much of the previous day trying to find out what time the game began on Saturday. The people I'd asked, mostly waiters, hadn't known or cared or felt like helping me find out. Three tabloid newspapers had been full of entertaining vitriol but no timetable. Even the television schedule was no help because coverage was perpetual. So I'd gone to bed knowing only that kick-off was sometime between three and nine o'clock (remarkably late but plausibly Spanish).

Many things probably happened in Barcelona and elsewhere on Saturday. Babies born, cars crashing, lotteries won, food drops in Africa and the discovery in Alabama of a piece of bark that looked like Elvis. All this passed me by, however, since I woke abruptly in soft fading light and discovered that it was just after five o'clock thanks to the miracle of time zones and jet lag. This certainly solved my worry that I might arrive at the Nou Camp some six hours early and be bored stupid. Now all I had to fear was showing up after everybody else had already gone home and with the Pesetero already aboard his luxury jet back to Madrid.

Cursing my incompetence, I skipped the coffin shower, grabbed my ticket and rushed downstairs, badly in need of a jolt of caffeine. Wising up after last night, I ducked into the first place I saw and had an excellent *Suissa* – like drinking chocolate mousse – and a slice of mushroom quiche. Not a pairing I'd recommend. At the Metro station I bought a fresh tabloid, which had another twenty-page diatribe against my man, plus a holier-than-thou editorial tucked in a corner saying that any protests ought not to escalate into violence, unless of course the perpetrators gave the paper's photographer an exclusive close-up of Figo's head on a stake.

Barcelona's Metro system is splendid: clean, fast and frequent. Once on my train I was surprised that I still seemed to be the only fan in town. Mothers with babies, teens hanging from the straps, old men reading papers, but no one looked like a partisan on their way to the field of battle. I re-re-checked my ticket to make sure I had the right week, and that the game was in Barcelona and not Madrid. The possibility that I'd slept through it was beginning to gnaw at me when we stopped somewhere and – finally – a bunch of recognizable football supporters jumped on.

You can always spot a soccer fan. The English louts of my past were pasty-faced, tiny-eyed, beer-bellied thugs, an insult to the very notion of athleticism in their nylon replica shirts. On the Tube, packs of them would all muscle into the same compartment and chant their nasty nursery rhymes about whose fucking heads they were going to kick in. This was Spain, so naturally everyone was far better looking and more fashionably dressed. But the edge of delinquency was there. Just to be going to this cauldron of an event, with its layers of love and hate, war and betrayal, was to admit that we still were, at our core, wild animals on the chase. It was going to be a scrap and we fans, in our tens and tens of thousands, had our own mission to carry out. And as promised, everyone but me was indeed armed with a whistle.

We surged out of the station. People milled in all directions, spilling out from noisy street bars and getting in the way of traffic. I couldn't tell where the stadium was and there was no single flow of humanity to latch on to. But striking out towards what seemed like a glow in the night sky, I soon spotted a dark mass up ahead, past lines of kiosks selling shirts and scarves. It was fairly impressive, although not the mega-cathedral of soccer that I'd been expecting. As I drew nearer I realized my mistake. This was the secondary stadium, presumably used for reserve team games and practice. Across the street was the real Nou Camp and, well, it was a lot bigger than a breadbox. I stood and gaped.

They hadn't actually unlocked the outer gates yet, but no one seemed too upset as we gathered amid soft misty rain. At eight o'clock the turnstiles opened and I made straight for the food stands to begin a scientific comparison of hotdogs of the football world. My conclusion: Barcelona might be about to get thrashed 5–0 (after all they were facing the European champions with loads of their best players injured, their seventeen-year unbeaten home run against Real had to come to an end eventually, and worst of all for Barça, the three previous times I had ever travelled over six thousand miles to watch a football match my team lost), but they served a mean dog – hot and meaty, no grease, a warm tasty bun, and zesty salsa that put fake bacon bits to shame. This would be a tough dog to top.

It took a while to climb all the way to the fourth level: nose-bleed price, nose-bleed location. I always love the moment of walking out from the concrete stairwell innards of a stadium into the bowl, with that first sight of the field of combat waiting below, brilliant green under the floodlights. Far below, in this case. Anyone with vertigo would be well advised to skip the Nou Camp. The place puts almost a hundred thousand bums on seats and gives every bum a breathtaking view through the classic principle of verticality. My feet were level with the head of the person in the row in front. The view was similar to watching on TV but the sense of hugeness, the rustling crowd, sparks of rain in the lights, a lingering taste of beef, the damp night air – all made it like nothing television can ever capture.

The seats were shiny plastic, each provided with a dual-purpose hole in the middle: rain drainage and a holder for rolled-up sheets of coloured paper. Apparently we were to hold up our squares upon cue. Coming from the great English soccer tradition I assumed we'd spell out 'fuck off, Figo' or something similarly sporting. It didn't take long for the stadium to fill. There was a general buzz of anticipation but almost no singing or chanting. Apart from a couple of densely packed sections of fans immediately behind each goal, who did seem to be on the verge of transforming into the kind of seething mass of fanatics you see in slow-motion promos for South American matches on TV, the rest were comfortable, middle class, well-dressed, thoughtful, somewhat dashing Catalonians. Plus me, of course, still trying to figure out when the game was going to start and imagining someone turning up to inform me that my ticket was a forgery and this seat had been in their family since Wilfred the Hairy, first Count of Barcelona, was killed fighting the Saracens in 898. (Legend goes that Wilfred's boss, the emperor, dipped his fingers in Wilfred's gory wounds and ran his fingers down his lieutenant's golden shield, as a mark of the hairy one's heroism, and thus was born the proud-in-defeat Catalonian flag of four red stripes on yellow, as worn tonight by the home team. Hopefully not an omen.)

A few minutes later, some people did turn up and take the adjacent seats, but to my surprise they turned out to be English. Later it dawned on me that we'd all been fleeced by 'Arry. My immediate neighbours were a jolly woman and her ten-year-old son, whose names I never found out since very Britishly we didn't introduce ourselves. They lived in north London and were lifelong Arsenal fans, eager to see two former Gunners who now played for Barça.

'They're both crocked,' I told them. The boy looked about to burst into tears. 'No sweat,' I lied, 'we're going to stick it to Madrid again anyway.' We? Kick my fucking head in if you must, but I was starting to feel the required spirit of partisanship before any big derby game.

Abruptly Real Madrid, wearing white, sprinted out on to the field to warm up. Instantly the drone of friendly conversation was shattered by the loudest, most piercing whistling from the entire crowd of a tenth of a million. It was horrible, even with fingers jammed in both ears. The ten-year-old next to me hunched over, visibly panicked. All around was a blur in the stadium floodlights as a sea of people waved white handkerchiefs. You expected the din to fade – surely people needed to breathe? – but the shriek went on unrelentingly for the length of Madrid's kickabout, the only variation being that the noise went from cacophony to complete bedlam when one particular white shirt kicked the ball. I'm sure that dogs in Morocco could hear it. The space shuttle probably wobbled from the shock wave as it passed over. It's hard to convey noise in words, but imagine someone standing next to you excitedly blowing a well-made metal whistle, the kind with a hard pea rolling around inside, the kind used by, well, referees for one. You'd find it unpleasant. Now multiply that shrill din by ten. Eye-watering, right? Now multiply that by a hundred. It burrows inside your brain and liquefies your spine. Multiply by another *thousand* and you start to worry that the piercing sound of it will shatter the stadium's foundations, possibly the earth's crust.

Meanwhile the Madrid eleven jogged, skipped, ran through one-touch routines, acting as if nothing unusual was going on (which in a sense it wasn't) but staying safely near the centre circle. After ten minutes they ran off quickly, in a tight pack, and the whistling stopped, leaving an eerie wake of quiet in which you could feel your eardrums throbbing. The message was clear: this wasn't simply blowing a raspberry at Figo, it wasn't even a broader protest against the invading Castilians, it was a dogged, cussed, unrelenting screw-you. We will not permit you to hear yourselves think for as long as you are here. We'll go on for ever, if that's what it takes, but you can't come here. I was ready to go home right then. It was enough, a preposterous venting of spleen, so that it seemed unnecessary to actually play a football match. The point had been made. Shortly afterwards Barça's players came out for their warm-up and got a smattering of mild applause. Perhaps the stadium was still shell-shocked from its heroic act.

Until now, my loudest experience had been a Christmas concert by the seventies punk band the Damned. They played a small auditorium with their amps turned up to eleven. I pogo-ed and threw beer cups while the Damned thrashed around on stage, spitting at the crowd. I went home with a wall of white noise in my ears. When I surfaced the next afternoon, the white noise was – if anything – worse. I stayed in bed. The next day my mother brought a cup of tea and demanded to know the name of the leader of this awful pop group who had recklessly ruined her son's chance of appreciating the finer points of Beethoven string quartets. She was going to write an Angry Letter. When I whispered that his name was Captain Sensible, she didn't believe me, but it stopped the Dear Sir plan cold. In any event, it didn't matter. Barça had Captain Sensible beaten.

At nine sharp, the two teams walked out together amid a jumble of whistles and applause. Then the sound system blasted out FC Barcelona's song, which is, effectively, the local national anthem. While everybody stood and belted out the lyrics, we all held up our coloured paper squares. Mine was red. I couldn't tell what the big picture was until I saw it later on Spanish TV – a complete and intricate heraldic Barcelona emblem. Ever the grand gesture. The song ended with a rousing 'Barça! Barça! BARÇA!!' and the players broke for their respective ends. All in all, and compared to 'We 'ate Totnum an' we 'ate Totnum' it was a pretty good call to arms. The game began.

Straight from the kick-off Madrid took the ball a few strides into our half. I was now feeling fully committed to the Barça cause, with no doubt about who was 'us' and who 'them'. I'm a gloomy nail-biter at big games, and I had an instant dread that we were about to be dismantled. However we got possession, a couple of passes and then a long ball launched towards our biggest star, Rivaldo, in space on the left side of Real's penalty box. Swept along with ninety-eight thousand people rising from their seats, I felt time hush and slow, like an instant replay. As the ball hung in the air, it was suddenly obvious to me that Rivaldo would be clear on goal. I could see what was going to happen next: he was going to score inside the very first minute. But by the time the ball arrived, a defender had closed down the space and the chance seemed gone.

Rivaldo controlled the long pass with perfect touch and took a quick flick to work around his marker – for me, this split-second of brilliance took an age. Then he was aiming to shoot, smack, the shot went off like a bullet, I heard the thwack of his boot on leather even though he was a speck at the far end of the field. Now time sped up again, the ball was a pinball, sizzling at goal only to be flapped away by the diving young keeper, Casillas. Where did it go? What happened? A choked roar from one side of the stadium, tricked by perspective into imagining a goal. From the rest a giant meaty 'Oooh!' – I'd heard it many times on TV and now I'd felt it for real – the resonant, throaty Nou Camp roar of approval. We all slumped down, limp and drained. The game was all of twenty seconds old.

The game settled down into lively cut and thrusts, neither side dominating. It was rough and tumble at times, but elevated by the ball control of players like Rivaldo and, it had to be said, Figo. As a midfielder the Pesetero was often involved, each time igniting a new volley of whistles. My sense was that the whistling was unnerving his team-mates more than the villain himself. Around the stadium I started to notice home-made flags and banners, various Figo insults. One was also a sing-song chant: 'Figo es cabrón.' I had no idea what a cabrón was, and the Brits around me were equally clueless. Then Barça hit the post. It was like that, out of nowhere a long shot coming in and ricocheting away accompanied by another deep 'Oooh!' Suddenly we were pressing them. And then we scored – a cross into the box, a header, nudged into the roof of the net by a stretching defender. It was all so quick and distant at the far end, but we were on our feet, roaring approval as Barça's players jumped at each other while the white shirts stood with hands on hips, and yes, it was really a goal, that momentary nag of doubt dispelled as the referee ran emphatically back to the middle for the restart. All right!

The breakthrough was liberating. Now there was more anti-Figo singing and a mild sense of carnival. As an honorary Barça fan for the night I relaxed too. Real Madrid just didn't seem up for it and you had to credit the crowd's intensity for part of that. It began to occur to me that Real was playing largely through the middle of the park, to little effect. I doubt it was explicit, but subconsciously, why would any of their players want to venture on to the wings, close to the hail of abuse and, I'm sorry to say, debris that littered down from the stands? One exception was Madrid's pacy Brazilian wing-back Roberto Carlos, who stood out for me as a class player among a galaxy of internationals. I'd noticed a swell of booing whenever he had the ball, and the young man in the row in front added enthusiastic monkey noises. It seemed Pavlovian really, Roberto Carlos touches ball, cue the racist mimicry. Pointless to mention that Roberto Carlos was a great player, he didn't ever abandon Barcelona, and Barça's current mega-star Rivaldo was also Brazilian. Racist abuse of 'black' players is alive and well in the world of soccer. I imagined kicking this youth in the head, which would have required minimal effort since my feet were right behind his skull, but would probably have led to my being hurled from the stadium hundreds of feet to the turf below. As it was, I'm afraid I did nothing other than mark this down mentally as a stain on my private rating of FC Barcelona. Hotdogs good, racism bad.

Half-time arrived soon after. Had every clear chance been taken, the score would have been around 3–1 to Barça, so 1–0 seemed about right. This is a common line of conversation about football – whether the actual score is 'fair' or not, which is odd since the game is designed so that frequently there is no connection between who dominated play and the result. The TV and newspaper people show scads of statistics these days: percentage possession, shots attempted, corner kicks won, and I suppose they do it because they have buttons on their computers that make it easy, but it's drivel. As any fan knows, one of the basic strategies for winning is to sit back, soak up pressure and pop one in on a breakaway. Many years ago I remember watching *Match of the Day* on the BBC where one mob laid siege to their opponents' goal and missed chance after chance after chance. I have never seen a more one-sided game. The other lot spent almost the entire match scrambling goal-bound efforts off their own line or hoofing the ball into the crowd, except for five hopeful breakaways on each of which they scored. Final score: 0–5. In what other major sport could that sort of travesty happen? Isn't it wonderful?

Half-time often allows the losing team to regroup and throw their opponents off their stride. Not tonight. Barça bossed the second half, knocking the ball around the edge of Real's box. Madrid, the most successful team in the world, were grim-faced and resigned, like Christians being thrown to the lions.

It began to rain, millions of tiny flecks slanting down and sparkling in the floodlights. Up went thousands of umbrellas, including mine, tricky in the tight confines. I discovered that if I tilted my brolly backwards water ran down my neck, but when I tipped the umbrella forward it dribbled over the racist below, which was much more satisfactory. He looked up at me once, but I acted oblivious.

By the last twenty minutes, Barça's stranglehold had relaxed a little. Just as it was beginning to smell like a 1–0, which is usually a marginally disappointing result, we had an attack that went from nothing to battle stations in two seconds. Perhaps I wasn't concentrating on the build-up quite as intently, but this attack was a great illustration of how what looks straightforward on TV can be chaotic to the fan way up in the sky-deck . . .

Suddenly someone is bursting through, in space. I think: it's Rivaldo, who else? He shoots hard and high, a scorcher, on target, surely a screamer of a goal? But no, the keeper saves it, palms the ball out, huge groan all around. My umbrella falls forward, making me momentarily lose the ball, which is dangling enticingly like a balloon suspended from the crossbar. Nearby players are moving towards it, the keeper's rising up from his save, but who's going to get there for the first thwack? One of ours! (Who?) He heads it. (Why?) It's as if someone hit a slo-mo button, the ball arcing lazily, possibly goal-bound but possibly over the bar. Everyone's shouting, arms up, urging it in. What's happening, what's happening? There's almost time to race down to the field and join the attack – surely some Madrid defender will intercept and belt it away. But they don't, they can't, as the ball glides across the line and drops in the net. G-O-O-O-L! The giant scoreboard confirms the second score of the night. More mad leaping, and I try to snap a picture while

25

holding my umbrella between shoulder and chin. The teeming rain makes the celebration seem wilder, although in truth this is icing on the cake and the game is well-won.

Back in the old days, when we all stood on terraces at football matches, goal celebrations were much more hazardous. You could easily surge down ten or twenty steps in the excitement and end up squashed against a railing. A friend once took me to see Newcastle play in London. When they scored a late winner, someone's punching fist of joy knocked off my glasses and I was down on my knees amid ecstatic Geordies singing 'The Blaydon Races', in despair at how on earth I'd get home with my six-inch vision. Amazingly I plucked my specs from a trash-strewn step uncrushed, and spent the rest of the game holding my face whenever the Toon pressed forward.

Although the fight had gone from most of Real's players, Figo, to his credit, wasn't done yet. Taking a pass in Barça's half, he accelerated goalwards dramatically and got off a hard shot, lethal-looking until a lunging defender deflected it away. Secretly I wished he'd scored, just to see how the stadium would have handled the tense final minutes. As it was, the fans cheered Rivaldo, who was replaced near the end, then sang a few more Figo ditties. Since there were no rival fans to taunt, apart from a sorry handful of Madridistas way up in the top row, the singing was patchy and it lacked the 'You're gonna get yer farkin' 'eds kicked in' edge I remembered from England in the aggro-years. Not that I had any business complaining, jetting in for the big game and wanting everyone else to sing for me, now 'we' were winning.

At the final whistle Madrid's players slunk away while Barcelona's hugged and pumped fists at each other. Consigning the capital's aristocrats to an eighteenth fruitless year at the Nou Camp clearly counted for more than another win-bonus. Rivaldo and Co. had no reason to magnify three points gained into some defiant gesture against the ghost of General Franco, but the historical echo was still there among the flags. The club song played again, we all stood and cheered, and that was that. Curtain down, show over, thank you and good night. As I made for the exit, someone tapped me on the shoulder and it was my neighbour the racist, handing me my dropped umbrella with a sweet smile. 'Gracias,' I managed. 'Visca el Barça!'

'Figo es cabrón,' he replied, for probably the two hundredth time that night.

'If you say so,' I said.

Plaça de Catalunya, at the top of the Ramblas, is the big rendez-vous after Barça victories. There were clumps of fans and plenty of cars and scooters with horns jamming, but the scene was relatively calm. Perhaps it was the rainy weather, but fanaticism in Barcelona seemed largely confined to the game itself. Before and after, people reverted to their day-jobs of being relaxed postmodern bon vivants. I decided to stroll down the Ramblas and find a tapas bar to top off a fine evening. Football matches are so enervating that whatever follows is usually an anticlimax. I followed my dropped-glasses Newcastle drama by going to the Albert Hall to hear Allen Ginsberg recite Beat Generation poetry. After the animal intensity, it was a huge bore. Sitting still was impossible. I wanted to charge the stage and rugby tackle the bastard.

Here in Spain, I wanted to at least practise my Catalan by ordering a few late-night jars. I marched past news-stands proudly displaying shiny porno mags at knee level and settled at Taxidermista in the Plaça Reial. Here, apparently, Miró and Dali used to come to get stuffed animals – before it became a cleverly named eatery, that is. The square was buzzing with conversation. Barcelona, I decided, likes itself. It has finally found its place in Spain and it's an inspiration. In contrast, few people are so lucky. People don't really 'find themselves', except in the movies. Instead we show up and plod along and sheer repetition usually carves out some identity or other. Tinker, tailor, left-winger, strategic planner. But who are we really? Life is as much a puzzle for me at thirty-nine as when I emigrated at twenty-six or when I didn't score against East House at thirteen. The best we can say is that if we're lucky we get a little more forgiving of how we turned out.

Afterwards, walking past the un-Erotic Museum I spotted a *gelato* stand. The young man who scooped my chocolate brushed away my local-speak in favour of his excellent English. I was still wondering about the man Barcelona felt completely unforgiving towards and, spotting a sports paper behind the counter, I asked him what a 'cabrón' was. He laughed and said there was no equivalent.

'But is it, well, sexual?' I asked.

He seemed confused, or maybe just embarrassed. 'It can have different meanings, good or bad.'

'So it's not wanker,' I suggested amicably, licking my cone.

'No.'

'Well, how about a goat then?'

'No, not an animal either,' he said and hurried to get my change.

My Metro home was full. A pack of pretty young girls was out on the prowl, clad in sparkling silver mini-dresses and painted eyes which demanded touch-ups at every station, as if the rattling train was responsible for progressive make-up degeneration. One forty-five, and this was easily the busiest Metro I'd ridden. My local eatery was packed and roaring again. I read the chalk menu twice while jiggling the door lock. *Botifarra amb mongetes* – sausages? – sounded mysteriously promising, but so did bed, five flights up, if I could ever get the key to turn.

Natalie couldn't say what a cabrón was either, when she picked up her keys the next morning. I lied and told her that I'd had a delicious dinner at the restaurant downstairs. What had I chosen? *Botifarra*, of course. Goodness, was that the time? I had to run.

The young Spanish computer programmer I sat next to on the plane, heading apprehensively for a month of training with Hewlett Packard in Portland, was only able to tell me that a cabrón was certainly meant as an insult in this context. In return I was able to tell him that I'd once been to a prison industry trade show in Portland and had enjoyed it very much.

Finally my brother-in-law, an American but with enough appreciation of football to name his cat Pelé, put me out of my misery. Figo went from Barça to Real? Is there any crime worse? There could be only one translation for cabrón in this case and it was obvious: the guy was a mo-fo.

Talent

The first bite was promising. A rush of mustard attacked my nasal passages, the meat hot and juicy, the flavour savoury. It seemed like a hotdog that might compete with Barcelona's, even if the bread was just two stale ends. But then came a crunch of gristle – upon examination it looked like a shard of bone – and my appetite withered. Fine, a little foot and mouth bovine spongiform to finish me off. I looked around for somewhere to spit and found a rusty oil drum half full of rubble. No, not a hotdog for the ages, and worse, it wasn't even a Sparta Prague hotdog, the whole point of this visit. A light rain fell as the dog-man folded away his poky little grill. The tiny crowd melted into darkening evening side streets and the remaining cops yawned and took off their helmets. I turned to Brett, who I'd dragged here from America with the promise of memorable life experiences, and shrugged hopelessly. 'Not particularly Bohemian,' he said cautiously, as if I might snap and challenge someone to a duel. I limped towards the tram stop. It was all massively disappointing.

The trip had begun, like many football matches, with so much promise. Brett and I found ourselves playing with retractable footstools in business class, courtesy of a generous computer in Heathrow. He works on the money side of the charity racket but he's also a complexity scientist, amateur jazz pianist, and lifestyle intellectual. You could accuse him of dilettantism I suppose, but Brett's problem is simply that he has a lot of talent and likes to combat boredom by trying new things. As the father of a witheringly intelligent four-year-old called Luke, Brett also knew that it was almost time to start coaching kiddie soccer back in Boston, so this was useful field research.

'Have you ever seen a double-crested grebe?' Luke had asked me on the phone a few weeks earlier.

'Double-breasted gleeb,' I mused. Some cartoon monster, presumably. 'Nope, don't think so.'

'Double-crested, not double-breasted,' the pre-schooler's voice corrected me impatiently.

'Oh, right.' I had no idea what he was talking about.

'They're quite prevalent out West.' (I kid you not.)

'Luke, could you get your Daddy to come to the phone now?'

Brett came on the line sounding weary. 'He's got this endless ornithology book with thousands of birds. Knows all their names. Every, single, one.'

Time to introduce that kid to the greatest sport in the world, I told him. Come to Prague and you'll see.

On the plane I gave him a preview of Sunday's big derby clash. 'So basically, Sparta and Slavia are the two top teams in Prague,' I explained, waving my wine-glass for emphasis as we burst out of Britain's five-hundred-foot cloud layer and into dazzling sunshine. It was wonderful being a subject-matter expert again. 'Sparta are over a hundred years old,' I went on, playing the age-card to my American companion.

'Then I guess they play a more sedate style of soccer,' Brett said over the top of a journal of chaos theory in which he is occasionally published. Like any good teacher I ignored him.

'They've won their domestic league thirty-four times, including every year in the 90s except '92 and '96. In 1996 they built a new stadium and basically went bankrupt, so they had to sell their best players to Germany and Italy. That's really how East European clubs are run these days – groom young talent then flog it to the big money leagues. Sparta dominates at home but they haven't done much when they compete against giants like Barcelona.'

'I see.' Brett was jotting notes that looked suspiciously like algebra.

'As for Slavia, they've won the championship sixteen times, basically whenever Sparta bottles it. Big glory days in the 1930s, when the Czechs were runners-up in the World Cup and Slavia had eight in the national team. They actually began as a sort of anti-Habsburg, Czech-language debating society in eighteen something so Slavia's always been the intellectual club, versus Sparta's working-class roots. Sparta's known as "the iron".'

'Up the proles,' said Brett, sipping champagne.

'When the students began demonstrating in 1989, Slavia's team gave pre-match gestures of support. There's a real political backdrop here. Slavia was actually dismantled by the Communists back in 1948 – they seized all their best players, wouldn't let them use their name and kicked them out of their stadium. Took them fifty years to recover.'

'Why?' said Brett, curiosity piqued by the unexpected class-warfare angle. Not something that particularly cropped up with his beloved Boston Celtics. 'Did the Communists want the working-class boys to win, the Iron Spartans?'

'Sparta,' I corrected. 'No, it's even better. The Czech army launched its own team in '48, they ended up being called Dukla Prague. During the Communist era they were dominant – eleven championships, eight cups. All the Eastern Bloc countries had army clubs that were basically the official team of the Party.'

'Why were they so hot?'

'Because any time they spotted a talented player, all they had to do was draft him into the army, then he had to play for Dukla. Sparta didn't do too badly as the workers' team, but the college kids got taken out behind the woodshed.'

'Not exactly fair,' Brett suggested.

'Didn't last, though. After Communism Dukla fell apart when the army gave up helping. They lost almost every game, got rele-gated, went bankrupt, got bought by a minor mogul, moved out of Prague to a small mining town and changed their name to Marila Pribram. Dukla Prague RIP.'

'Leaving us with the intellectuals back from the woodshed versus the unemployed iron workers.'

'Just like it was, bourgeoisie versus proletariat, pure capitalist-class conflict on the soccer field . . .' I rhapsodized.

'. . . And our allegiance will be?' asked Brett, nervously fingering his monographs.

I felt my ears pop as we began to descend. 'Whoever's playing at home,' I said. Brett looked confused. 'Better quality seating. Better odds of winning. Better odds of being part of the delirium of victory. Better odds of not getting beaten up.'

'I'll drink to that,' said Brett.

Prague airport was modern, full of ads for entities like Accenture, empty of any sign of class conflict. Amazed at our competence we managed to change money, find the bus stop and decipher an elaborate ticket apparatus where tickets were valid for differing lengths of time depending on what hour of the day it was. Soon we were on board and sloshing through wet suburbs.

My traveller's radar noticed that there was an astonishing ratio of attractive young women to all other age-gender cohorts. (A work colleague called Dominic once informed me that he had counted one hundred women while walking through a park in Brussels, and only one was cute. Brussels thus scored a miserable 1 per cent on what became known in our geek-filled office as the D–BOM – Dominic's babe-o-meter. Sexist, callous, statistically suspect, but once you knew about the D–BOM it was hard not to use it. Prague I reckoned at a stellar 30 per cent.) Brett clearly had made the same scientific observation, since his chaos monograph was nowhere to be seen as he hung nonchalantly from a strap near the door.

When the bus terminated we followed a gorgeous gaggle of Czech girls down to the Metro platform. Curiously a digital clock showed not the time until the next train, but minutes since the last one. This seemed a gloomy Iron Curtain metaphor, but I couldn't get Brett interested in it. Meanwhile more pretty young things boarded, dressed to kill. It was Saturday night and boho Prague seemed ready to party.

Despite all the stations being called things like 'Hradčanská' – simple straightforward Prague place names, but they all blur together to the dopey jet-lagged traveller – we found our way to Wenceslas Square, which is just a wide central shopping and banking street. An immediate looming view of the vast lit-up stone castle on the hill made us stop and stare.

'And there's McDonald's,' said Brett, pointing. 'There's always a Mickey D's. Homogeneity. Lack of species diversity. Reduced adaptiveness.'

'But can't you sense it?' I countered. 'It's Kafka's Castle. The Defenestration of Prague. *The Unbearable Lightness of Being.* Havel and the Velvet Revolution. This is a ground-zero town.'

The rain eased as we walked and the old town's grand and crusty façades were all dizzyingly reflected in puddles among the cobbled streets. It was Mozart-ville, it was Mittel-Europa, it was historical and alive all at once, and it was heady and wonderful. And tomorrow the classic historic schism that sliced Western industrial societies in half during the twentieth century – the class of brains against the class of brawn, white against blue collar – would be redrawn in the form of the beautiful game, where, I felt, a post-Marxist synthesis of both would be needed for ultimate victory. Or so I thought.

My air of elation was buoyed yet further as we crossed Old Town Square past the famous astronomical clock where a procession of carved figures pop out of cuckoo-clock doors to accompany each hour's chimes. Despite the weather a few cafés had covered seating on the square and I started to anticipate bringing the first foaming Pilsner to my lips. Just then two girls came up to us, cute of course, and one of them said, 'Tu van sayks?' There was a momentary pause, while my brain double-checked its dictionary to make sure I had heard correctly. Mistaking our gob-smacked dumbfounded-ness for serious consideration, the other girl sought to clinch the deal by pouting like the next Pamela Anderson. 'Good sayks,' she added, slightly plaintively, as if she suspected us of imagining that the sex would be desultory and boring.

Brett broke the spell by laughing and we hurried on to our hotel sign burning welcomingly across the way, pursued by a volley of blown raspberries, which I confess I found rather endearing. What a town: picture postcard buildings and cute girls offering sex to total strangers (with British Airways Club Class baggage tags).

Reception was a little bizarre. My cheerful 'We're here for the big game,' was met with raised eyebrows. And though it was mid-evening we had to pre-order breakfast immediately from photos of various combinations of eggs, yoghurt and coffee which didn't seem to be meaningfully different. Then the lift was so tiny that I doubt a single moderately plump person could have fitted inside. In contrast, our suite was so vast that we kept discovering new rooms throughout our stay. We dumped our stuff and contorted ourselves back down in the lift, ready to join young Prague on the make.

After strolling through delightful car-less streets we had an eclectic dinner at a club called Delux. The interior was rococo, the food Thai, and the central dance-floor given over to energetic salsa. It was all good. Only the beer was local and that, of course, was excellent. 'How's your son?' I asked Brett over an Irish coffee. He rolled his eyes.

'Luke is a wonderful challenge. Thank God I got three days off.'

'You can thank me.'

'He's probably going to be the next Harrison Birtwistle and it'll be all right, but he's walking around the house all day making these *horrible* squarking noises.'

'Grebes,' I said sympathetically.

'Oh no. We're off birds. He's composing music. But he's got it all in his head and he doesn't hear the noises coming out of his mouth. He stands there and says, "What do you think, Daddy? That was in the style of Gershwin." Goes on all day. He's driving us insane. We can't send him off to other kids' houses because he's only got three friends and two of them have gone away and the other one refuses to play composing.'

'Fair enough. Who's Harrison Birtwistle when he's at home?'

'A composer. Avant-garde, atonal. Brilliant but challenging. Squarking noises, basically.'

We continued the musical theme after dinner by sampling one of many classical concerts on offer. Prague is the town of Ave Marias. No Harrison Birtwistle here, just easy-listening classics for the punters. Wolfie Mozart may well have been a true genius but I nodded off in my chair next to the wall.

I had one of my most memorable musical experiences with Brett. We were in Nairobi for a few days around Christmas, just after barfing at fifteen thousand feet and not making it to the peak of Kilimanjaro. I blamed taking an altitude sickness pill called Diamox which had the dramatic side-effect of making my mouth fill with foam every time I drank a beer. We made a giant warning sign out of stones halfway up the mountain that said 'Diamox–Schmiamox'. The real problem was probably the single word our wrinkled local guide kept chanting every day: 'polé, polé'. *Slowly*, he was always reminding us. Trained in the financial canyons of London and New York, we were climbing far too fast. Or maybe there was something nasty in the mountain water we'd been drinking.

On the hike down we held a disgusting stories competition. Brett won. A friend of his had been trekking in the Himalayas, way above the tree line, staying hydrated from bubbling streams of icy melt-water. A month later he was back in Washington DC, at a diplomatic black-tie party. Sipping a tall gin and tonic he was holding court to a cluster of women in cocktail dresses with tales of watching dawn break at twenty thousand feet. Suddenly two of the women screamed and a third, bug-eyed, pointed past him and fell over backwards. Glancing over his shoulder he couldn't see anything wrong and so he hurried off to the bathroom to check his face. He set down his G&T on the marble basin and squinted at himself in the mirror. No caviar in his moustache, bow-tie on straight. Nothing. He turned on the tap and cupped his palms with cold water to splash his face. That's when it happened. There was a sudden twitchy feeling, a quick slurping sound, and the front six inches of a four-foot long and very thirsty tape-worm dropped out of his left nostril and took a noisy gulp of water.

Anyway, back in Nairobi we stumbled across one of those amateur *Messiah* singalong performances in the local Anglican cathedral. Come one, come all. We joined the rump ex-pat community for the night and pitched in. 'Gloria, Hosanna in Excelsis' turns out to be a lot trickier than 'Glory Glory Man United'. Faced with a big fat songbook and a panicky conductor mouthing the words at us, I lip-synched my way through, camouflaged by a hundred better singers and full orchestra. At half-time I badly needed a beer and spent the next twenty minutes hidden behind my songbook, furiously swallowing residual Diamox foam. But then came the Hallelujah Chorus: one place you can really let rip. As we belted it out I was so excited that my voice gave up singing altogether and was simply laughing with giddy pleasure.

Brett nudged me awake as 'Sheep May Safely Graze' was ending. Aware that we'd fallen into a kind of 'Prague is for lovers' honey-trap that was completely on the wrong end of the class struggle, we gave up for the night, resolving to gear up for football first thing in the morning. No sex crossing the square this time – maybe somebody else had scored.

Breakfast arrived at six. Brett showed it into our palatial kitchen, ate a mouthful of ham while I slept and then went back to his room. Around nine-thirty we both surfaced to cold coffee. I fetched the paper and studied the sports pages. There was lots of coverage of Sparta–Slavia of course. 'Slavné derby nadchio fotbalový národ.' Photos, quotes, highs and lows of the great rivalry, and something about a 4–4 score-line. My guess was that some pundit was predicting an exciting game, but I had a nagging feeling that something was getting lost in translation. 'Páteční remíza 4:4 se zařadila mezi derby, na která jde stěží zapomenout.'

'Any idea what a zapomenout is?' I asked Brett, who was clicking through TV channels for the top-rated Prague station where the weather forecast is presented as a striptease: the more they take off, the hotter it's going to be. It was time to get professional help. I rode the lift down to reception.

'We're looking forward to seeing the Sparta–Slavia football match today,' I smiled. More raised eyebrows from the frosty lady behind the counter. 'Do you know what time it begins?' She grabbed my newspaper and stabbed her finger at the *Fotbal* page. 'Zapomenout?' I tried.

'It is finished, finished,' she said, spitting the Fs. 'It will 'appen last night. No more. Finished.' And with that she retreated into the little back-office where hotel reception people hide and send telegrams and other useful things.

This was like being hit on the head with a dumb-bell in a Laurel and Hardy film. I tottered out to the street in a daze and found a coffee bar where a kindly and knowledgeable Czech *barista* gave me a coffee and explained all. Yes, the games are all scheduled for each weekend. But every week, one match, usually the biggest, is shown live on TV on Friday night. Taking me for an American he said, 'It's like Monday Night Football, only the other way round, no?'

'So it was last night?' I repeated dully.

'Yes. It is backwards.'

'Bugger it.'

'Say this again?'

'And the score was?'

'Four against four. Amazing, no?'

The pain from the dumb-bells began to throb. I'd come six thousand miles only to miss the big event. I'd dragged someone else all this way to show him the real thing and I'd messed it all up. I was a cretin. And we'd even been here, eating Thai food and watching pretty Czech girls dance salsa, when we could have been at the stadium watching the class struggle. And worst of all, the time I have an American soccer sceptic with me, we don't get the usual 1–0 bore, but an eight-goal thriller. Eight goals? How was I going to break this to Brett, happily tucking into congealed omelette upstairs? I'd have to kill myself.

Actually, Brett didn't mind. Football might be my excuse, but he was thrilled just to be in Prague. He set down a heavy-looking book called *Investigations*. 'Let's wander the Old Town,' he said, 'then go catch some other game after lunch. It's going to be a nice morning. Warm.'

'Some other game?' I gaped at him. 'We can't do that. This is the only game that matters. Everything's ruined.'

Miserably I looked in the paper and found that Bohemians Prague, very much the third club in town, were entertaining a team called Viktoria Plzeň. According to the paper, Bohemians languished in an uninspiring tenth place out of sixteen in the Fotbalová Liga, while good old Viktoria Plzeň, with just two victories against twelve crushing *plzeňs*, propped up the bottom of the table. Disconsolate, I pushed my plate away.

'Hang in there,' said Brett. 'Let's check out the castle and then find a good bar.'

'And get drunk as fast as possible,' I said, a true football fan.

I wandered through the most beautiful city in Europe with my nose in *The Rough Guide to European Football*. Following lengthy details on the trophy lists and ultra-culture at mighty Sparta, struggling Slavia and defunct Dukla, came a brief 'what else can we think of' section called Groundhopping. I learned that Bohemka play at a much-loved tatty little ground engagingly called the Dimple in a working-class neighbourhood. Their history, according to the guide, was 'blighted'. Curious, I thought. (We crossed the Charles Bridge.)

After a tour of Australia in 1926 they acquired a bizarre kangaroo logo. During Communism the club even played for a while under the memorable moniker Spartak Stalingrad. They never won anything until 1983, their miracle year, when they bagged their only championship and made it to the semi-finals in European competition. They almost won the league again two years later when scandal hit with the arrest for fraud of a club functionary. (We walked up the hill and around the castle.)

A period in the wilderness followed and Bohemians finally got relegated from the first division in the late nineties. But the plucky little club bounced back and even snagged a British insurance company as sponsor. Now the Bohemian kangaroos have an old-fashioned red double-decker in which to parade around town. According to my guide, near the stadium were two bars: the Eva Bistro, where home fans sink Staropramen pilsners from someone's living room, and the U Tří Soudků, over by the away-fans enclosure and thus often 'full of mean Moravians on match day'. (We passed through a large cathedral with bright stained-glass windows.)

'Let's get lunch at a non-touristy place,' I suggested, having recovered some enthusiasm for life.

'Someone told me about an amazing cellar bar,' Brett offered.

'We probably ought to head over near the Dimple.'

'But this is the best bar in the world. It's right around here.

Halfway up the hill to the castle on the right somewhere near the American Embassy.'

I checked my watch. 'All right. We can have a Staro there first.'

Given the vagueness of our directions, we resorted to a mine-sweeper approach of trekking up one hillside street and then down the next. 'It's not the search algorithm with the best odds,' said Brett as we puffed uphill for the third time. Despite seeing dozens of embassies and hundreds of inviting cellar-bars, the American Embassy remained elusive, even after getting some 'second left, third right, round the square, down the alley, second cobbled courtyard, you can't miss it' directions from a strolling policeman. Idiotically I had arrived in Prague wearing tight lace-up business shoes, and the combination of aeroplane feet-swelling and puddle shoe-shrinking was starting to create severe ambulatory discomfort.

'Who told you about this place?' I grumbled, needing a villain to take my mind off my blisters.

'Buddy of mine,' said Brett. 'Works at the Santa Fé Institute. A quality guy.'

'I'm sure he's a complete delight.'

'No, I mean quality's Brad's thing. Optimizing manufacturing systems, amazingly precise process mapping, six sigma error rates, you know . . . He's world class.'

'But not so amazingly precise with directions, this Brad?'

Brett snorted. 'He likes his beer. Probably out of his gourd the entire time he was here.'

Abandoning all hope of finding the best bar in the world, we spotted a tram that appeared to go near a street name that seemed like the address of the Dimple in my book. Since no one on the tram looked like a Bohemians fan, we were lucky to see the stadium through some trees. As we hopped down, a huge crowd roar swelled on the breeze, stirring my heart with resurrected hopes of class conflict. Excited, we followed our ears down an empty side street and half an hour before the scheduled kick-off found ourselves outside a locked and deserted stadium. Just as the Rough Guide promised, it was indeed tatty. Solving the mystery of the vociferous crowd, someone turned off a tape playing over the loudspeakers, leaving sudden silence but for a few distant cars and birdsong from the trees. There were still no fans to be seen. A poster on the wall indicated that the newspaper was wrong – kick-off was not for another hour and a half. I looked around hopefully, a little unnerved by the fake crowd noise, still half expecting to see a throng of chanting supporters marching up the hill, but there was only a handful of helmeted cops leaning against a concrete wall, eyeing us with mild curiosity.

'Lunch,' I said.

'Is that Eva place near here?' Brett asked.

'I don't know,' I said, and then spotted the chaos gleam in his eye. 'Sorry, I can't walk any more. Let's go in that place on the corner. It's got a beer sign.'

The mean Moravians were probably the giveaway. They didn't exactly all stop talking when we came in and hung up our coats, since they appeared moodily quiet to begin with, but they did all stare at us through the cigarette haze and they weren't smiling. The back room only had three large tables so we had to find empty spaces by pointing and looking hopeful. We took the shrugs as 'what the fuck, sit where you want, but don't piss us off any more than we already are, you capitalist fucks', and sat down gingerly. A barmaid brought plastic menus and sure enough, we were in the U Tří Soudků. Although we were violating my rule of being home fans for the day, it was too late to back out. I pointed at a giant poster of Staropramen.

'Dos,' I tried, indicating Brett and myself. The woman ripped off a chit of paper and slapped it in front of me. I fumbled for coins but she'd already gone.

'Why are you speaking Spanish?' Brett asked.

'Shh,' I said and hid behind my menu. This proved to be completely unenlightening. The sports pages in the paper had words like 'fotbal' and '4:4' but here, nothing sounded anything like any food item I could think of. We were on another planet, outer-Moravia at least. Giggling from behind the other menu suggested Brett was reaching the same conclusion.

The waitress came back with two frothy beers and poised her

pen for our order. 'Inglese?' I said, cringing. She shrugged. The men all watched us like Dobermann pinschers in a bad mood.

'I'm going to order completely at random,' said Brett, somewhat predictably. No one else was eating anything we could point at. 'That, that, and one of that,' Brett said. The woman looked at him incredulously, the way one might look at someone who has just ordered banana–yak milkshake, a party platter of one hundred sea cucumbers and a bowl of burnt molasses. I noticed that one of his choices only cost five crowns. It was probably a pat of butter.

'Get something else,' I urged.

My own scheme was to point to the most expensive thing on the menu and stop there. This time the woman nodded. For all I knew it was Moravian haggis, but at least my choice didn't make me a laughing-stock.

'Cheers,' said Brett, taking a long pull at his beer and emerging with a foam moustache.

'Good luck,' I responded.

Through the window I still couldn't see any fan activity, although a van drew up and out came a dozen more cops in full riot gear. Precautions are sensible, especially in football, but this seemed overkill since there were no visible fans at all. The mood inside the bar, however, seemed to be getting noticeably more tense. But that was probably due to us.

We ordered two more Staropramens using our favoured pointing technique and sat in companionable silence. (It seemed safer.) When the food came, it was clear that 'you get what you pay for' beats 'random' when ordering from indecipherable menus. I had a chicken breast in a congealed sort of sauce and about thirty tiny croquette potatoes. It tasted just like you'd imagine and went very well with the beer. Brett's plate had a heap of grey bread, the pat of butter I'd predicted, and a slice of cold potted meat, origins unclear but something in the words of the menu made me suspect the head of a particularly unfortunate beast. It glistened with wobbly edges of aspic jelly. Images of rotting animal carcasses danced before me and I stabbed a potato quickly. To his credit Brett gave his meal an honest try, before admitting defeat and cadging a few croquettes from me. 'Good plan us ordering different things,' he said. 'Classic Edgeworth Box risk mitigation strategy.'

Then it happened. Commotion on the street outside. Some lads crossing the road – nothing obviously wrong – but the riot police, now thirty or more, seemed to perk up, form a block, edge forward. A few shouts, more twitching from the cops, and then a pod of them darted at the trouble, visors down, clubs out. A quick mêlée in the street, shouts, two men down, blows raining on them, their mates scattering, a police van squealing round the corner, lights flashing, the head cop talking into a walkie-talkie, coordinating his troops. Brett leapt up, glad of the chance to escape his head-meat, and called back from the window, 'They're really beating on that guy! He's down. They're dragging him away.' I cringed, hoping that our Moravian pals inside didn't decide that we, capitalist Yankees, were on the wrong side of the metaphorical barricades. This was clearly not a football match worth getting beaten up for.

It was all over in two minutes. Calm returned. The streets emptied again. The silent pilsner drinkers continued to sip away, staring into space. We polished off the croquette potatoes, smiled and shook our heads at the waitress. The bill came to about four pennies so we left a guilty tip and skedaddled. Outside it had begun to rain, but at least it looked like the stadium was now open for business. As we crossed the road towards a line of riot police, fresh from their triumph over two sad-sacks who had crossed in the wrong place, Brett decided it would be fun to take their picture. More baton twitching and for a second I feared he was next for the paddy-wagon, but maybe his obvious patina of 'I'm just visiting from the good ol' US of A' saved us. 'Don't do that,' I hissed, secretly thrilled we had a record of these thugs.

Given the success of my restaurant tactics, I bought the most expensive seats that Bohemians had to offer, and we went through the turnstiles. The Dimple is small; 'stadium' is far too grand a word for it. The place only holds seventeen thousand, of which three get to sit down under a rusty roof. Our seats were in the very top row (the seventeenth) about a third of the way along the touchline. At one end the home fans massed behind a goal, possibly just huddling together for warmth. Four of them had drums and they made periodic attempts to arouse their comrades into chants but with limited success. Someone had hung a banner over the fence that proclaimed 'Tornado Boys', adding yet another nickname to the team's collection. Among the usual banners for Coca-Cola, pilsner and cigarettes, one said 'Fotbal ano Drogy'. In the far corner was the infamous away enclosure. I counted twenty-one fans in it. Presumably they would have been twenty-three strong but for the intervention of Prague's finest. Either way, it didn't look like mighty backing for cellar dwellers Viktoria Plzeň.

'Well, it's not what we came for,' I said.

'Very modest,' said Brett. 'Low key.'

'Hints of class conflict. You know, scandalous urban bohemians against coal miners, or whatever they do in Plzeň.'

'Very subtle hints.'

I sighed. 'Not one of the high temples of soccer, anyway.'

'More like my back yard.'

Now I looked, the pitch did not seem remotely fit to host a football game of any level. A man in overalls was trundling around the edge of the field with a contraption that laid a fresh line of white paint on the grass. Its guide wheels kept sinking beneath the surface and leaving troughs. Large pools of water lay on the saturated surface. Each penalty area was a mud-bath. Bohemians' goalie, busy practising, looked like an urchin, caked from head to boots. Every time he dived, he'd slide an extra couple of yards into a puddle. Women wrestling in mud – entirely possible here, but a serious game of football looked highly doubtful.

Nevertheless the teams trotted out at three o'clock to a small round of applause and the game began. In the main stand, which was two thirds full, everyone sat back and stared morosely into the middle distance, much like our friends back in the bar. Obviously this wasn't a match for chanting, cussing out the ref, baiting the away fans, or urging on the Tornado Boys. This was a match for getting through.

The ball developed a magnetic attraction for various pools of water scattered around the field. Whenever a player raced forward, ball at his feet, one or other puddle would seem to suck him in and then stop the ball dead, until two or three other mudlarks arrived simultaneously in a spray of brown to thrash the ball away. I'd had hopes of a fast one-touch passing game, ball on ground, the kind of skills shown recently by the Czech national team and the best Czech players like Nedvěd over in Italy, where the money is. It wasn't to be. The level of talent on display here was marginal to start with, and the muddy conditions immediately reduced the match to a ruckus in the park.

After four minutes Bohemians scored with a sharp shot that I barely saw. I caught myself looking round for a video screen to watch the replay – but the sponsors' generosity had ended with the old double-decker parked side-on behind a goal, so we could all see the insurance company's advertisement. At least everyone stood up and there was a jolly, single cheer. Then it was back to puddles and staring into the middle distance. Only the twenty-one Plzeň fans, I noted, had any passion for the game. In the manner of true fanatics who don't care that their team is pitiful, bottom of the league, already losing today's match, they were far from downcast at the early goal. Most of them had taken off their shirts and were cavorting like stoned hippies at an old Grateful Dead concert. Far too much Staropramen, in all likelihood.

Twenty minutes passed slowly. Brett looked at his watch. 'What's the most bored you've ever been?' he asked.

I pondered my many choices for a while. 'Probably a summer job at a Dickensian company called Wood Engineering,' I decided. 'Helping Big Al on the glueing machine. He fed in slabs of compressed particleboard, the machine glued strips of veneer along one side, and I stacked the slabs on a trolley. Four seconds a plank. When we finished a batch I wheeled the trolley ten feet back to Al and he'd feed in the next side. The best part was mixing brown gunk and white powder into skanky glue.'

'What were you making?' said Brett.

'Table tops. The last month they let me work unsupervised and I built a huge teetering stack and then clocked out for good. Later

I heard that every single table was rejected for sloppy veneering. The company went four legs to the sky.'

Below us a Plzeň defender tried a long throw-in and fell in a puddle. 'They went bust because of you?' said Brett.

'I like to think I contributed. Anyway, it was impressively boring. Why do you ask?'

'Oh, no reason.'

I resorted to lecturing Brett on the offside rule, since this is always a perplexing issue for people new to the game. Most matches have a few marginal offside decisions which often have a dramatic effect on the outcome, since breakaways result when the flag stays down. The rule itself requires an astute appreciation for imaginary, moving parallel lines across the field, which have to be interpreted – in an instant – by underpaid amateurs who are themselves running up and down the touchline, with other things on their mind. (Like whether to get chicken breasts or potted head-meat in jelly on the way home, judging from many of the decisions they end up making.) If the offside law is an ass, its quaint method of enforcement is a recipe for disaster. Technology could of course be deployed to make better decisions, but instead of this, technology is deployed only to criticize the decisions after they have been made. Not so good for football, but great fun for the TV industry that funds the game. What else would the commentators have to talk about if not for dodgy offsides? Was he on or was he off? It's all so Heisenbergian.

In any case, Brett perked up and was soon quibbling with the officials. Given the quality of play, I was glad he had a distraction. On the field it was becoming clear that Bohemians had a few nippy and skilful players who, in drier circumstances, might have dazzled us with some fancy footwork, before being sold on to Sparta or foreign big-money clubs. Viktoria Plzeň were artisans by comparison and began to accumulate yellow cards for assorted lunges and clumsy tackles, inevitably into sheets of water. Their manager worked up an excellent froth of outraged victim-hood at each card, flailing his arms and stomping in his own puddles just in front of his little bench.

'This Plzeň team,' said Brett, testing his emerging critical appreciation for the game. 'I mean, basically they suck, right?'

Instinctively I leapt to the away side's defence. 'They're never going to win but most of them are reasonably competent. I've seen plenty worse teams.'

Played for them too. By the time I was sixteen I had sunk to a school team made up of asthma sufferers, druggies, the congenitally overweight and the alarmingly tearful. But our opponents one windswept afternoon looked just as implausible and I remember clapping my hands encouragingly at kick-off, confident that we would win. We lost 22–0. This remains my all-time heaviest defeat and even our indomitable house master, who was known for keeping up an owl-like cry of 'shoot! shoot!' whenever his boys had possession of the ball, was reduced to a telling silence.

That 22–0 drubbing was an extreme example of a regular problem of mine: aspirations dwarfing ability. I desperately wanted to be good at football but I was mediocre. I scraped at a violin for six years of what must have been cruel punishment for my family. I sliced golf balls from our front garden into oncoming traffic. I wrote poems that no one must ever see. It's not that I'm an utter failure, as I've come to realize from the sadder wisdom of adulthood. It's just that I'm like most people – we don't have any special talent. All it means is that if we want to narrow the aspiration gap, we have to sweat like pigs. Genius, on the other hand, is effortless. Maradona with a ball, Midori with a fiddle, Tiger with a club, Dylan Thomas with a pen: these people simply know what to do.

Plzeň had one particular player, a forward, who I began to follow. At first this was for want of anything better to do, and because his ponytail made him stand out among the other short-back-and-sides. Gradually I realized that number 15 never, ever managed to touch the ball. His journeyman team was getting out-played but the rest of them were at least getting stuck in. My man was merely in the vicinity, frequently making a run to the left as the ball was sent right, taking it upon himself to stand near Bohemians' goalkeeper when he was holding the ball, and then trotting busily back to centre-field. I wouldn't say that he was necessarily useless, a really useless player in a pretty useless team, but he was decisively ineffective. In this beer and sausages version of football – no glamour and affected heroism within a mile of the Dimple – the ponytail was a mistake. Had 15 been the best player on the park we could have forgiven him, but he was poor, pretending to look useful while not really wanting to get muddy. Secretly, I sympathized.

The fairest I can say for half-time's entertainment is that it was heartfelt. The crackly loudspeaker introduced a busty local pop star called Dina, who appeared beneath us at the edge of the field, clad in leather jacket and stilettos, image triumphing over practicality. Dina tried to tiptoe a few yards on to the pitch, holding a large old-fashioned phallic microphone whose cord snaked back worryingly through the puddles. She turned to face us all and immediately sank backwards three inches into the mud, almost toppling over as a guy in a seventies tracksuit rushed to help. It was riveting. Everyone stared down at her, willing something bad to happen.

Music started up on the speakers and Dina, having now planted her stilettos like tent pegs at a wider spread, raised her arms to signal louder. The boost wasn't enough and she waved for more. This time the distortion was deafening – you could feel the concrete steps buzz, and Dina launched into her song while frantically waving the volume down again. For three minutes she managed a gyrating, raunchy sex-goddess routine from the waist up, while keeping both legs stock-still and anchored in the ooze. The crowd, about 99 per cent male, watched quietly with intent hopeless lust. She deserved bonus points for sheer pluck.

After her song, Dina got to present a prize to one lucky lottery winner, a boy who reminded me of Shaggy from *Scooby-Doo*. We couldn't tell what the prize was until Dina enlightened everyone by mimicking unzipping her leather jacket, to wolf-whistles from the peanut gallery. Sure enough, it was a copy of Czech *Playboy*. 'Hi,' said Brett, 'I'm Dina. Have a picture of me naked and spread wide.'

Half-time did not help Plzeň. Already down a man when one of their defenders was defenestrated for yet another over-lusty lunge into a puddle, they went further behind four minutes into the second half. It was an excellent goal too. One of Bohemians' speedy forwards took a ball in the centre circle, feigned a pass as the Plzeň defenders pressed up for offside ('no way!' shouted Brett), and then raced the length of the field, letting off a shot just as a defender reached him on the edge of the box. The ball flew into the roof of the net and everyone cheered for ten seconds. Then we all sat down again to watch the rooftops fade into purple twilight, and with it the hopes of Plzeň's twenty-one topless pogo dancers. Fuelled by Staropramen, I felt strangely serene. World-class derby match no, but all this muddy effort was no less genuine.

'What was that book you were reading this morning?' I asked Brett. 'Musings or whatever it was.'

'*Investigations*. It's some new thinking by Kauffman about complexity,' he said. 'You know how the fourth law of thermo-dynamics is basically entropy? Order breaks down into chaos unless new energy is put into the system.'

'Right,' I said doubtfully. Below us a Plzeň attack broke down into chaos as if to illustrate.

'Yet we find so much order in nature, in biological systems. It's paradoxical.'

'So what's the answer?' I said.

'Kauffman, he's quite the guru, reckons he's come up with an entirely new corpus of physics.' Bohemians' goalie whacked the waterlogged ball upfield. It rose briefly into the grey sky and then arced predictably back to earth, directly into a puddle, very much the old corpus of physics. 'Newton and Einstein were wrong, Kauffman argues. Physical systems like, say, the people in a bio-sphere act as their own autonomous agents. They affect their dynamic environment as well as being affected by them. So you can't pre-state the configuration space. Algebra-like rules go out the window.'

'I never liked algebra.'

'Think about how the genetic code itself has evolved – all those random cell divisions and re-combinations – changing the transformational rules of the biosphere itself in ways we could never have predicted from the starting point. So you have to reassess how you define what life means. It gets pretty complicated.'

'Of course it gets complicated,' I sniffed. 'It's supposed to be complicated. It's all about complicatedness, you said.' Two Plzeň defenders ran for the ball and crashed into each other. Given a sudden free shot on goal, Bohemians' forward blasted high and wide.

'So maybe there isn't one simple answer,' said Brett. 'That's why the book's called *Investigations*. It's a homage to Wittgenstein who wrote a really significant treatise with the same title.'

'And what was that about?'

'Objectivism. Metaphysics. He was trying to come up with an entire new language system, a nomenclature that was completely non-subjective.'

'What, like Esperanto?'

'No, not like Esperanto. Look, I'll lend you Kauffman if you want.'

'That's all right,' I said. 'I'll just scan the back cover.'

Halfway through the second half the skies opened again. The poor Tornado Boys behind the goal ran for cover in the corners. Within a minute about half of the announced crowd of 2,460 had disappeared. The twenty-one Plzeň fans didn't care – they continued leaping around, faces skywards, in religious ferment like Hare Krishnas on a day out. Then Plzeň scored a goal, a soft one since the ball stopped in a puddle right in front of Bohemians' goal and for once, a Plzeň player was in the right place to poke it into the net. Rapture for the twenty-one and a few groans in the main stand, but the mood of stoic introspection wasn't much disturbed. As the rain eased again, the twenty-one started a tiny wave of their own, over and over like piano keys tumbling down, order imposed over entropy, while in the sky above them a soft rainbow shimmered briefly.

It seemed too much to hope that we were in for a grandstand finish. Plzeň weren't really up for it and sure enough Bohemians added a clinching third goal when the Plzeň keeper dropped the slippery ball and watched it smacked into the net by someone named Dvořák. As the can-can boomed incongruously over the speakers, the goalie went from being annoyed with himself (fist-bashing in puddle) to embarrassed at his blunder (sitting in puddle, head in hands) to cover-up and denial (racing after the referee back to midfield to claim a foul, for which he received Plzeň's umpteenth yellow card). Who'd be a goalkeeper, anyway?

And that, pretty much, was that. Brett was by now abusing the linesmen for their overly subjective offside calls, the Plzeň human wave had slumped and put their shirts back on, and the ref was looking at his watch. It hadn't been much of a day for class conflict, although the State had beaten up a few beery louts for the sake of the Bohemians. Nor had we witnessed anything remotely like a top-class match between bitter rivals. But this was honest, ordinary, healthy community football and I'd enjoyed it. As the referee blew for full-time, the Bohemians team formed an orderly line and trotted around the edge of the field, smacking hands with their fans. It wasn't triumphal and neither players nor fans were getting too excited, but it was good to see.

I limped down from row seventeen behind Brett and we milled around behind the stadium, on the off-chance something might happen. Already the red double-decker was edging out of the gates and slipping away into the evening. It doesn't take long for a crowd of two and a half thousand to disappear back into a city, but there were still a few hangers-on near the hotdog stand, just a charcoal griddle on a rickety table. The greasy aroma tickled my nostrils and I was instantly ravenous. They were down to one last dog and a crust of bread, but the price was right and anyway I was too far-gone on grass-roots authenticity to listen to Brett's potted head-meat warnings. I slathered mustard the length of my sausage and took an enthusiastic bite.

A few months later, to make amends with Brett I took him to see a real big match – Barcelona's last home game of the season at the Nou Camp. Despite beating Madrid, Barça had suffered a rotten season, winning nothing. Of course they had sacked their manager. One of their players had failed a drugs test. The fans were in whistling mood again. Tonight was salvage time for the club as well as me.

We downed tapas and jugs of sangria before the game. It was a blustery June night with massive dark clouds hanging symbolically over the stadium. Just as in Prague, we sat in the very top row (except this was twenty-two flights of steps high), and watched through binoculars as the cavernous place slowly filled up. To squeeze into next season's Champions League, Barça had to beat a tough Valencia team and all game long they didn't look remotely like managing it.

I had brought a book of my own to inflict on Brett, revenge for *Investigations*. It was called *A Mathematician's Apology*, written by a Cambridge maths don called G. H. Hardy in 1940. Happily Brett had never heard of it. Hardy was apologizing for the apparent irrelevance of pure mathematics to the challenges of daily life. How could you justify a life spent in abstract theory? Hardy doubted that you could. His slim apology also told the story of how in 1914 Hardy brought a poor, young postal clerk called Ramanujan from Madras to Cambridge, where they published five brilliant papers together. Then Ramanujan fell sick and died of tuberculosis, aged thirty-three. Possibly Hardy blamed himself. But most telling, Hardy realized his limitations. He was a very, very good mathematician, in his own words, 'for a short time the fifth best pure mathematician in the world'. Yet raw untrained Ramanujan was in a class of his own and Hardy saw the gulf. Aptitude and effort were no match for an innate gift.

'That's what frustrates me,' I told Brett. 'The gap between being competent and being brilliant is so big. It's daunting.'

'And there's nothing you can do about it,' Brett said, shaking his head. 'Except be satisfied with yourself.' He smiled. 'And applaud.'

With eighty-nine minutes on the clock the score was 2–2, two wonderful pot-shots from bow-legged Rivaldo keeping Barça in the hunt. But a draw was no good. The *socios*, cold and subdued throughout a poor game, began to groan and whistle as their team ran out of time and ideas. You could taste the bile welling up. And then soccer does what it does best: it knocked our socks off. A hopeful last-minute ball arrived somewhere behind Rivaldo, his back to goal and eight blue-shirted defenders all around. He took it high on his chest and dropped one shoulder. Bicycle kick. Twenty yards. Screamer. Bottom corner. Hat-trick.

Delirium around the stadium. Thirty thousand swept past a few dozen bemused police on to the grass, cavorting, hanging from the bending crossbars and forming conga-lines with flags, horns and flares. Brett and I jumped on our chairs and joined the mass worship: 'Ri-val-do, Ri-val-do!' The damn Barça song boomed out as firecrackers exploded like bombs in the night. We were laughing, agog, ecstatic, tingling at the image of that last kick and Rivaldo racing away, peeling off his shirt.

Reuters called the goal a Rivaldo master-class. Writing for the *International Herald Tribune*, Rob Hughes said it was 'as graceful as the purest silk' and suggested that it could be worth fifty million euros to the club in Champions League money. Rivaldo himself, very much the artist unable to explain, thought that his goal was 'nice'.

In the top row of the Nou Camp we were still elated. 'What a shot!' yelled Brett, converted. 'He's a total hero, a genius. I'd go anywhere to see him. Anywhere.'

That's right, my friend, you would, you should. This is it. This is why we come.

Extremism

Listen to my friend Paul, an ex-pat Scot who produces TV commercials in Hollywood. 'There's nothing like an Old Firm game. Drink yourself stupid, shout about how you hate the Pope and loathe all Catholics, behave despicably all day. Nothing like it.'

'Do that nasty song,' his wife, Sharn, eggs him on. 'The coming round the mountain one.'

'Oh, I cannae.' He's stone-cold sober and six thousand miles away after all.

'I will then,' she says. And she does.

> Could you go a chicken supper Bobby Sands?
> Could you go a chicken supper Bobby Sands?
> Could you go a chicken supper, you dirty Fenian fucker,
> Could you go a chicken supper Bobby Sands?

She turns to me in appeal. Butter wouldn't melt in her mouth. '*That's* what they sing.' For the uninitiated, Bobby Sands was an imprisoned IRA member who went on hunger-strike until he died. Martyr or terrorist, take your pick. But a Catholic either way.

Paul is an American citizen these days. He rarely goes back. And he's not even the right religion – he's Jewish! But as a true-blue Glasgow Rangers fan, he won't have anything green in the house and his views on the Pope are colourful. He watches every Gers game on satellite at a smoky Scottish pub in Santa Monica even though this means being on his barstool at four in the morning – LA-time for a Scottish kick-off at noon. At half-time they have sausages and bread from a greasy plug-in hotplate – delicious and highly authentic. Afterwards you can see them staggering into the bright California dawn. There's never any trouble because the

Celtic ex-pats watch at a different Scottish pub miles away. And their songs about the Queen are just as nasty.

This was clearly far more than a mere game of football. When Paul's father, Harold, called from Glasgow to say he'd managed to buy two tickets in a safe part of the stadium, I was thrilled. And for once I'd have no trouble with the travel logistics: familiar food, local currency, a common tongue.

'Watch yourself,' said Paul.

I saw my first tartan kilt at Glasgow Central Station, shortly before my first blue Rangers top. The kilt was on a pixie lassie in punk fishnets and Doc Marten's, yammering into her mobile – modern Scotland, I suppose. In the station hotel lobby, the woman on the desk wasn't offering welcome smiles. 'Chicken?' she said, narrowing her eyes.

'Beg pardon?'

'Are ye chicken in?' She handed me a pen. 'Fullinthis and sayne here. You have a name?' I told her I did. My brother had already paid for our rooms but she wanted my credit card for 'incidentals'. I asked if I could possibly have a non-smoking room. 'Ah've no idea,' she scoffed. 'You'd better *loook* it up. And which paper shall you want?'

'What are my options?' I asked.

'All o' them.' Her pen twitched impatiently over my guest card. 'Your heart's desire.'

'I'm sorry but I'm not from around here. I don't know the names of the newspapers. Which has good football coverage?'

'Fitba?' She gave me a searching glance. 'Ooch, I don't know. Probably any. The *Herald* then?'

'Lovely,' I said.

No one tried to carry my bag. The corridor was as long as a train platform and smelled colourful. Eventually I reached my room and struggled for five minutes as my plastic card-key fought against a rusty old lock, finally bursting in on the smallest room I'd ever seen. There was a thin single bed and a desk parked along one wall, while a veteran television filled up most of the free floor space.

Cells in Alcatraz were more spacious. I peered through my window down on to a street lined with nightclubs and chip shops, neon signs flickering in warning like a classic film noir. Following an old superstition of mine, I tossed my bag heavily on to the bed and stood back to watch.

Some years ago I met a girl who looked a little like the singer Cher with big black hair. Driven by a memorably passionate late-night, whisky fuelled kiss on our previous encounter, I visited her during a massive ice storm with every intention of scoring. It looked as if we might be snowed in for the weekend. When I arrived I made straight for her bedroom and chucked my bag possessively on her bed. Nothing happened for about three seconds and then the bed's legs collapsed noisily and comprehensively. I was rattled. She was irritated. We ended up in a home improvement centre hunting for replacement brackets and the only screwing I did that weekend was with a Philips cross-head.

My hotel bed did not break, suggesting, I hoped, a more high-scoring weekend. I was so impressed at the uncompromising tininess of my room that I lay on the floor crossways, just to see if I could. That's when Toby pushed open the door and peered down.

'Six feet,' he said. 'Mine too.'

'Hi,' I said, scrambling up to give my younger brother an awkward English hug. It had been a couple of years. We had a lot of catching up to do.

'When did you get here?' I said.

'Just now.'

'Good journey?'

'Can't complain.'

'Hungry?'

'Could be.'

'Walk first?'

'All right.'

We set out in twilight and walked away from the station. I immediately liked the feel of Glasgow. The central buildings were solid but elegant, late nineteenth century with the soot scrubbed off, grey stone and neat rows of windows that got smaller as they went up. Traffic noise echoed from the walls. Pubs and restaurants were already giving off that welcoming evening glow against a darkening sky. It was cool and damp. People were walking fast. It all felt purposeful and decisive. I tried Toby again.

'How's your work going?'

'Keeping busy. You know.'

That's the thing about Toby: he's extremely low-key. 'So what exactly have they got you doing?' I asked.

'Data security mainly. Our network's a bit of a mess.'

Or rather, he's a low-key extremist. During his twenties, for instance, Toby concentrated ruthlessly on sleep. When I phoned my parents, they'd invariably whisper apologetically 'Rip Van Winkle's asleep'. I would observe that it was mid-afternoon. 'I know,' my mother would sigh. 'I took him some tea after lunch but it just goes cold.' He would hibernate until dusk most days, and then appear briefly to consume cornflakes and fend off nagging questions about expired driving licences and unpaid bills. Our parents, desperate to become people with grown-up children who were now free to go on cruises with other grey-hairs, tried faking university applications on Toby's behalf, to no avail. Van Winkle just wasn't interested in waking up. He was preoccupied with comatoseness, to the exclusion of all else. Eventually, he'd banked so many hours of accumulated rest that he can now stay awake almost indefinitely. Black-belt sleep nirvana.

'D'you have a title these days?'

'Oh, yeah.'

'What is it?'

'Something about telecoms. It's on my business card some-where.'

Nowadays his focus on work is just as extreme and unswerving. All he does is work, not apparently for big money or lofty status, but because it's how he does things. Our parents, in between tropical cruises, now complain that they never hear from him. We should all have seen this single-mindedness coming, mind you. As a small boy he would eat food clockwise around his plate: all the peas, then all the potatoes, then all the horseradish, then all the gravy, finally the beef.

'Can I get one of these business cards? None of the numbers I have for you ever work. Ironic, really, given your job.'

'Got one somewhere.' Toby rummaged through his wallet unconvincingly. 'Must be at the hotel. Give you it later. Oh, I found this clever mobile for you too. Works anywhere in the world if you stick a sim in. Except I forgot it. I'll send it to you.'

My sister likes to tell people about the year she invited Toby for Christmas. He was due around mid-morning for presents but never showed up. The turkey and trimmings were ready by early afternoon and soon drying out. Eventually everyone sat down and Toby's Christmas cracker went unpulled. Worried stiff, she called all his numbers throughout the evening. The next morning there was still no sign and after tearfully making turkey sandwiches for the kids she was about to call the police when he strolled in and plonked down two mobile phones on her kitchen table. 'Our network's been crashing and I've been flummoxed trying to sort out why,' came the explanation.

'We've been worried sick,' my sister spluttered. 'You're twenty-four hours late for lunch. You could have called. You could have called twice!' Toby looked thoughtful. Obviously it hadn't occurred to him.

I was about to propose dinner when we noticed a walking tour of the city called Ghoulish Glasgow, led by a Gielgud lookalike clad all in black. We paid up and tagged along behind a dozen school kids and a lovey-dovey couple. As the sky shaded purple, our guide led us around Glasgow's old tobacco mansions telling tales of slit throats, bubonic plague and the Hellfire Club – rich young trouble-makers who burned down a church. The theatre on the same spot today has one stairwell perpetually colder than the other. ''Tis the ghost of the poor child burned alive in the flames,' hissed mock-Gielgud. The kids shrank back from him. A few started whimpering.

One of Toby's mobiles beeped. It was Harold, making arrangements to meet us with the tickets before tomorrow's game. We

57

settled on the John Greig statue outside Ibrox, commemorating the 1971 disaster when Rangers equalized in the last seconds and sixty-six fans on Stairway 13 were crushed in the chaos. Plenty more fans have been killed in brawls at Old Firm clashes since then, but 1971 was by far the worst loss of life at a single game. How would we spot Harold? He was bald and he'd be wearing a Rangers top.

Our tour snaked down narrow passageways that smelt of urine. Victorian slums, built for immigrants as Glasgow's port boomed, according to the man in black. Many were Irish, escaping famine. Glasgow was, he said, a rough tough working town.

'That's how it began,' I told Toby as we dawdled behind. 'The Old Firm isn't just a football rivalry, it's got all this baggage of religion and politics.'

I'd posted a question on an amateur Rangers website asking what made the Old Firm unique. BigBiffa replied that it was the only derby match in the world where one of the teams (i.e. Celtic) did not represent the country where the game was played (i.e. Scotland). Mac69 jumped in to correct him. Both teams were equally part of the United Kingdom of Great Britain *and Northern Ireland*, and thus subjects of the Queen. Someone else angrily demanded that everyone lay off the politics. BigBiffa said he was just answering some guy's question and it was a free fucking country. The war of words spattered on. I felt like a trouble-maker and logged off before someone blew up my computer.

Meanwhile Gielgud was recounting something horrible about milk. 'Milkmaids came along this very street carrying their pails every morning,' he proclaimed, waving his umbrella at the children for emphasis.

'Ever been over there?' I asked Toby.

'Ireland?' He hesitated. 'Once or twice.'

'It really all began way back in 1167,' I said. 'Feuding Irish chieftains encouraged the English to invade and start colonizing. Then 'Ennery the Eighth imposed Protestantism and gave the best lands in Ulster to Scottish settlers. One-nil to the Unionists.'

'I know,' said Toby. 'Eventually Catholics rose up and massacred the Prods, 1641, one-all. Cromwell counter-attacks, 1649, two-one. James the Second becomes Catholic king of England, 1685, two-all. Nobbled by William of Orange at the Battle of the Boyne, 1690, three-two.'

'How do you know all this?' I asked peevishly.

'How did people know the milk was fresh?' asked Gielgud.

'Its sell-by date,' Toby heckled.

Gielgud ignored him. 'From the rich froth on top o' the pail.' We were all standing in a dark alley next to a tower where they used to hang suspected witches. It was starting to get chilly.

'Rangers have a load of Dutch players in their squad,' I said, attempting to shift the point of attack. 'A couple of years ago all their fans wore orange to a cup final against Celtic, instead of the usual patriotic red, white and blue. Orange, mind you.'

'We did this stuff at school,' said Toby.

'But sometimes the poor milkmaids would be left with unsold milk at the end of the day.'

'It was the Home Rule movement, wasn't it?' said Toby. 'When the Troubles really began. The Protestants around Belfast saw themselves as hard-working successful Anglo-Saxons. The Catholics in the Irish south saw themselves as Gaelic and independent from London. Both sides formed militias. Political crisis. Penalty shoot-out. First World War. Irish independence. Protestants control Ulster. Unionist discrimination. Civil rights movement. Frustrated Catholic expectations. Orangemen marching season. Violence flares. Battle of the Bogside. British troops.'

'I was reading somewhere that Rangers' table-tennis tables are blue,' I said, swimming hopelessly against the tide.

Toby ricocheted on like a ping-pong ball. 'Sectarian murder. UVF and IRA. Tit for tat. Internment and torture of IRA suspects. New street demonstrations. Bloody Sunday. IRA bombs.'

'So they'd chop up rotten bits o' meat and scatter the scraps into the milk.'

'Fall of the Stormont parliament. Direct rule from London. Bobby Sands. More bombs. New Northern Ireland Executive. Problems decommissioning weapons. And so it goes.'

'You're no fun at all,' I said. A vast store of unlikely knowledge was classic Toby.

'And overnight the rotten meat scraps would decompose and give off gas which would rise as bubbles and create a wonderful new froth on the milk the next morning. Nice fresh milk and no one any the wiser when people drank it and fell sick.'

The loving couple stopped snogging. The kids looked unnaturally pale under a street lamp. The tour broke up and I didn't notice anyone giving a tip. Toby, thankfully, appeared to have finished. I suggested we scare up some dinner. 'I've got a restaurant recommendation.'

'Not from him, I hope,' Toby said, waving at the departing actor.

'From *The Rough Guide to European Football*.'

Toby laughed. 'What is it, a chip shop?'

'Actually, sort of.'

We rode one of Glasgow's miniature underground trains to the city's 'most famous restaurant' – The Chip, but it was full. A kindly waitress directed us to a wee place nearby but we couldn't follow her directions properly amid the hubbub, so we got lost in side alleys. Two other restaurants looked promising but were jammed. We picked up another hot tip and this time took a taxi to be safe, over a hill and past the university. Plenty of empty tables here but they were all being held for the nine-thirty diners. We wandered down the street and sniffed at a modest Italian. Full. On the corner was a great bar, they told us. We followed the pounding music around the corner but their kitchen had stopped serving three minutes earlier. We took another taxi back to the centre of town, jumping out when we reached a street lined with eateries and pairs of bouncers on every door. A tapas bar looked enticing but had thumping heavy metal and a two-hour wait. A pub had a sign saying 'no colours' but promised 'fresh tavern fayre' inside. I couldn't understand the man on the door but his shaking head was clear enough. Across the street a Cuban-themed club was just folding away its tables for dancing.

'What's going on?' I shouted at a waitress. 'Everywhere's packed.'

'Saturday night, end o' the month,' she said. 'They all got paid. And it's no' even started yet.'

We ended up in an all-you-can-eat curry house. Cliques of girls were walking past our window in sequins and tight dresses, hair teased up, flirting their way past doormen in oversize black suits. We knocked back Kingfisher and ate vivid red rogan josh and naan bread while the street life grew ever noisier. Coming out near midnight we made for the station and our hotel. As we walked around a crowd jostling at a velvet rope, a sharp-dressed man staggered out of the door, bounced off me and doubled over in the gutter.

'Bad milk on *his* cornflakes,' said Toby.

The rock and roll was almost as punishing in my room three floors above so I turned on the television and perched on my bed. Scottish pundits in comfy chairs were discussing tomorrow's game. I watched for twenty minutes and realized that I hadn't understood a word of the brogue.

The world's smallest hotel room came with matching bath towel, roughly the size of the colour magazine in the *Sunday Herald*. Sitting with damp hair downstairs in the breakfast room I devoured the sports pages. There might be no visible build-up in the city, but the press was full of the Old Firm. Gers' manager would be in trouble if the Bhoys beat them again. The title race could be all over after ten games. Raised on a rich diet of championships and cups, Rangers fans were frustrated. Key players had been sold and not replaced. It was high time for Norwegian forward Flo to deliver, just like Celtic's Scandinavian goal-machine Larsson. Someone had left an *Irish News* on a chair. Its front page was devoted to Unionist terror on the streets of Belfast, the back page to an exclusively Celtic perspective on the upcoming 'battle'. Old Firm glory was secondary to winning the title, said the manager, which was only half true. Underneath was an ad for an arduous-sounding coach trip from Belfast to Celtic's upcoming game in Norway.

No sign of my brother, so I nipped up to his room and clouted the door. He peered out wearing shorts, with a mobile phone against his ear and looking tousled, a man who'd been up all night.

Toby is good-looking in a casual, rugged, blond way. I expect that when he completes his decade of work he will devote his forties to relationships, one after another, maybe three simultaneously, and he'll probably be extremely successful at it. Our parents will complain that they can't keep up with the names of all his girlfriends.

'You'll just have to re-boot it, Alec,' he was saying, holding up five fingers at me. So I returned downstairs and piled up a full Scottish breakfast. The hacks were unanimous that Rangers were in trouble. A glorious decade of dominance was a memory and supremacy had slipped across the Clyde. Harold had sounded just as gloomy on the phone, telling us that the pub after the game would be 'something – but only if we win'. This lack of confidence was widespread and surprised me, even if it was sensible given Celtic's current swagger. Hang around most clubs and you'll see people gnawing at their fingernails. Pessimism is rampant. Faith in the team is equivocal. It's a doubting sort of faith because everyone knows that, unlike the Almighty, the centre forward is horribly fallible. But I'd imagined that supporters as fiercely proud as Old Firm loyalists would have unshakeable religious faith in their team. After all, Rangers have won the league *forty-nine* times. But in the papers, on the web, in bars around Ibrox, the Bears were having a crisis of faith. At least unless they beat Celtic today.

Toby appeared opposite me, holding a plate of glistening sausages.

'Did you get *any* sleep?'

'Enough.'

'And is Alec going to be able to manage without you for a few hours? You can't be on the phone during the match.'

'As long as our firewall stops misbehaving.'

I studied him, trying to figure out what was wrong. At last it dawned on me. 'Don't you have anything blue?' He was sporting a beige hooped rugby shirt. Might as well have a bull's-eye on his back.

The taxi-driver sighed when I asked for Ibrox. I gave him my story about seeing the greatest games in the world but he only shook his head slowly. Why a midday Sunday kick-off, I asked?

'So they cannae drink. Except they all drink at home, so it doesn't stop anyone drinking if it's drink they want. The drinking's how it all starts. Aah, the demon drink.'

I looked out of the window. The shops were all shuttered and police stood on every corner. It was rainy and the street was filling up with people heading for the stadium, a few now risking showing their Rangers blue tops, none with Celtic green on this side of the stadium.

'They don't look too bad,' I said. I was starting to feel that this 'clash' (the papers' favourite term) had become weighed down by its own shadow. Every single person we spoke to had a warning. Every fan was transformed into a dangerous bigot. Weren't they just people too? But the statistics were genuinely grim. Since their first game in 1890, Celtic and Rangers have played each other about three hundred and fifty times. Rangers hold a slight lead. Off the field there had been eight murders just in the previous five years and the number of arrests for assault throughout Scotland triples on Old Firm days. Our taxi dropped us off and U-turned without waiting for a tip. We were on our own, surrounded by people all donning the colours, working up to the season's first ninety minutes' hate.

While we waited for one of the forty-five thousand people now wearing a Rangers shirt to become Harold, we checked out the merchandising. Outside on the road the amateur stalls had some of the more brazen stuff. 'Bears against Bigotry' said one T-shirt. 'Teach a Tim the sash' — that being an auld Protestant dance. 'No Surrender to the IRA' another proclaimed. Inside the Rangers shop things were squeaky-clean corporate. It was like a fast-flowing Gap store during a blue month. A sign over the exit promised that all profits would be invested in players and the registers were humming. If you didn't fancy another De Boer top, you could always buy a brick with your own name on it. Since Ibrox was constructed in red brick, this canny ploy seemed to have vast potential.

Back at the John Greig memorial I made eye-contact with a bald guy the spitting image of Paul. It was Harold. We ambled down to the far end where two police lines kept the blue and the green

63

armies throwing distance apart. Things were noisier here – the baiting corner, Harold called it. I was hoping that our seats might be near this frontier territory but they turned out to be in the opposite corner of the Club Deck, safer and quieter. 'Just as well,' said Harold. We thanked him and went in.

Ibrox is the cleanest stadium I've ever visited. I realize that there are higher accolades one could bestow: I know a Frenchman who suffered through an English summer camp as a tortured, introverted fifteen-year-old and the only prize the sporty counsellors could find to give him at the 'everyone's-a-winner' awards ceremony was for having kept the cleanest horse. Like the personalized bricks, many seats had also been sponsored by fans, and they'd certainly packed them in tight. Ibrox reminded me of that old pork-marketing adage: sell every bit of the pig except the squeal.

We were high up, almost in the rafters. To our right was the Rangers end and away to the left was a sea of green and white striped scarves from ten thousand Celtic fans, doing a good job of asserting territory. As I watched, they unfurled a big Irish tricolour and let it billow on top of them. Rangers' response was a round of 'Rule Britannia'. No doubt about it, the atmosphere was tense. The gusts of hatred coming off each end were palpable. It was like sitting directly between two loudspeakers and fiddling with the balance knob. To the right:

> Follow! Follow! We are the Billy boys
> Follow! Follow! You'll know us by our noise
> And if you follow Celtic then we'll chase you til you die
> Cos we all follow Rangers.

To the left:

> We don't care what the animals say
> What the hell do we care
> For it's all we know
> There's going to be a show
> And the Glasgow Celtic will be there.

I'd prepared for the game by watching some Scottish football on television. It wasn't very good. The chasm between the Old Firm and other teams verges on the ridiculous. I watched Celtic stroke the ball around – twenty, thirty, forty passes in a row while the lads from Hearts scampered like puppies. The thirteenth time Sutton tapped the ball to Lambert the commentator grew weary of stating the obvious and fell into companionable silence until some time later the move ended. 'Oh, it's gone out,' he said, as though waking from a long nap at the seaside to find that it was low tide. Minutes went by one second at a time, the fans applauding occasionally at a back-heel or quick one-two. This wasn't a football match at all, more like formation dancing, or a group basket-weaving demonstration.

Rarely have I sat through a more lopsided, and thus boring, football match. And that's what you get in Scotland, year after year, two decent teams yawning their way through match after match with an endless procession of no-hopers. Dundee, Kilmarnock, Hibs – it's like eating a box of Liquorice Allsorts: each one looks different but they all taste the same and after a while you just feel sick and fed up. There's a smart-alec English website that shows the Scottish league table with Celtic and Rangers at the top and then every other team listed identically as 'Jocks'. Thank God for the Old Firm derby.

At noon the teams ran out quickly and with no provocative national anthems, no dangerous delays, the match began. It followed tradition: too fast, little guile. Even the many non-Scots playing for both sides seemed caught up in the wildness. Rangers in particular were poor. They had most of the possession, but they were porridge going forward. Celtic did nothing at all, except score a goal from a long free kick that somehow bounced through the goalie. Celtic chanted abuse while the Rangers end fell quiet, as if their speaker cable had frayed loose. I sat there dozily, drifting off. For some reason Celtic's goal carried me away to an altogether more innocent soccer song I hadn't thought about in years:

My old man's a dustman, he wears a dustman's cap
He took me round the corner to see a football match.
Fatty passed to Skinny, Skinny passed it back
Fatty took a flying shot and knocked the goalie flat.
Where was the goalie? The ball was in the net
Halfway up to heaven with his trousers round his neck.

Around seven years old, my friends and I sang this all the time. In those days we lived in a village near Birmingham. My brother hadn't been born yet. I see the song like a cartoon: the ball blasting into the keeper's tummy like a cannonball, his eyes popping out like gobstoppers. Quite how failing to keep out Fatty's pot shot qualified him for the Pearly Gates First Eleven, well, Lord knows . . .

Back in our village, my old man actually worked for Mobil Oil. He was in sales, but I believed he drove one of the big red tankers with a flying horse on the side. I supported West Bromwich Albion back then, simply because my father had stood on the terraces at the Hawthorns for years. Unlike the dustman, he never took me to see them play, but I still ran weeping to my bedroom when the teleprinter revealed that they had lost the League Cup final in 1970. My unimaginative best friend supported Man United. We had our own version of one against one in the back garden, theatrical cup finals between Albion and United played completely in slow motion, a mesmerizing new gimmick of televised football in those black and white days. We ran in slow motion, shot in slow motion and dived slowly to tip the ball against the apple tree goalposts.

My parents sent me to Sunday school, probably so that they could read the paper in peace. It wasn't as much fun as slow motion football, but we did get to sing 'All Things Bright and Beautiful' and colour in drawings of Gentle Jesus and the Disciples with fat waxy crayons. It was a quiet, safe village, so I would walk home alone. One day, two bigger boys on bicycles stopped me, grabbed my scripture picture and jeeringly crumpled it up. Then they pushed me into a bank of stinging nettles until I was wailing. At

66

home my mother rubbed my blotchy legs with dock leaves and took an iron to Jesus. My dad sat me in our Vauxhall Cresta and we set off in hot pursuit of the bullies. We found them cycling along a few miles away, and he hooted as we passed. Toot-toot. I was crestfallen. I thought he was going to give them a smack (what I got for impersonating the BBC weatherman in crayon on my bedroom walls) or run over their bikes or at least get them in trouble with the village bobby.

Years later, I'm amazed how painful this puny memory is. It happens to everyone, of course. I discovered that the world was a little bigger than I thought, a little more scary. Bad surprises sometimes happened. My old man couldn't always make it better. As for Gentle Jesus, where had he been in my moment of need? Completely meek and mild, passive and useless. I decided then that I didn't have any faith in God, whether he existed or not, although I didn't dare tell anyone and still muttered my prayers at bedtime.

Some people follow a club because of their religion. Others follow a club as though it were itself a religion. It works much the same way. You love the place madly and totally. You attend every weekend, year after year. You sacrifice for them – costly midweek trips to the wrong end of the country. You worship them – kissing the club emblem on your shirt like a rosary, pinning up posters on the walls. You donate to them – sponsor a brick instead of the steeple restoration fund. In return the club does nothing at all. It barely acknowledges your existence. Then you die and, if you're lucky, your ashes are sprinkled in the centre-circle in front of forty thousand empty seats.

Half-time was an improvement over the actual game. While Toby carried on an agitated phone conversation with the hapless Alec, I browsed through Rangers' bilious fanzine *Follow, Follow* ('unoffical, unauthorized, uncensored and unashamed') and counted the different ways it described Celtic supporters: Tims, junglies, shower of shite from across the Clyde, Mhanky Mhob, Great Unwashed, Soapdodgers, Beggars, Sellick and Yahoos. But this was nothing compared to the venom hurled at Rangers' chairman, manager and half the team. Money-grubbing, lazy, demotivated,

67

tactically clueless, antifan and past-it. A pair of Rangers fans next to me were on much the same wavelength.

'We're total fuckin' shite.'

'No fuckin' clue.'

'Mols isn't even fuckin' fit.'

'Klos lost the game for us already.'

'Nothing but fuckin' arm-waving from De Boer.'

'As usual.'

I ventured that I was impressed by Ibrox.

'You should see Celtic Park.'

'A fuck of a lot of money went in there.'

'They're on the right track.'

I suppose nine titles in a row would spoil anyone. The grass was looking mighty green across the river.

The second half was piss-poor, except for a five-minute period that was almost worth the price of admission by itself. Rangers were just starting to threaten an equalizer, shots flying in, when Celtic countered at speed. Swede Larsson skipped past Dutch Konterman and was through on German goalkeeper Klos when the last defender, Italian Amoruso, smacked him down. Penalty! Gloating in the green end and a massive shoving match in the box, theatrical and excessive. Two players ended up staggering together into the net. Off went Amoruso, but when Celtic's lead brawler only got a yellow the crowd was incensed. A Rangers player helpfully punted the ball high into the stands to show how he felt. Larsson lined up the penalty amid outrage from three sides of the ground. It looked good but goalie Klos dived and beat it away to the biggest roar of the afternoon. The penalty had been a fair call, but a wave of vindication spilled around Ibrox. A let-off. God was a bluenose after all.

The stereophonic chanting swelled again. From the right end:

> We are Rangers, super Rangers
> No one likes us, we don't care
> We hate Celtic, Fenian bastards
> And we'll chase them, everywhere.

It was too noisy now to hear the Celtic response properly, but the Irish tricolours were waving again and the repeated 'orange bastards' was unmissable. On the field, the soccer had gone postal. Studs flying, injustice piling on injustice, baying from both ends, the game barely more than a Highland ruck. Toby glanced up from his hand-held computer, where he was furiously tapping away at a network diagram that was flashing alarmingly. Could Rangers' ten men turn their escape into new confidence, find the equalizer, go on to forge a famous victory? No, they could not. Not even close. After nearly boiling over for a few moments, the game fell back to a dull simmer. Celtic had a few chances as Rangers left gaps, but didn't take them. With five minutes to play, Ibrox was thinning out rapidly. Since it was still only 1–0 I was amazed how hard Rangers were finding it even to get the ball near Celtic's goal. The green end was starting to celebrate an away victory:

You can talk about your great defenders
Sing and shout about your No Surrender
But let us give you this wee tip
We'll be there for the league and the cup
Rangers bye bye.

In injury time, Celtic finally put the game away. It was a sweet low shot that curled into the far corner, right in front of the green army. As Celtic's manager raced euphorically from his dugout someone on Rangers' bench threw a bag of ice at him.

Walking along the Paisley Road among subdued Rangers supporters, Toby and I came across a rusty van selling sausages and chips. The aroma was compelling. I ordered a portion of chips and splashed salt and vinegar until the paper began to disintegrate. They threw in a deep-fried sausage for free since it was the end of the batch and we walked along in soft rain quietly feeding our faces. The deep-fried sausage was a miraculous thing – the crispy batter outside collapsing on to juicy meat within. Perfect for a damp Glasgow afternoon.

'How's that firewall holding up?' I asked my brother.

'Not well,' he said.

After half a mile we reached a Rangers pub. Harold knew the manager and had asked him to let us in as a favour. The place was seething and there was a bouncer guarding the door. 'Full up, lads,' he was calling to the throng around the door.

'I'm Giles from Los Angeles,' I told him. 'Danny was told about us.'

'And ah'm Tom Cruise from Hollywood,' said the bouncer, chummily.

It took a while to get Danny to the door and he was hesitant to let us in. He rubbed his chin and blew out air before grimacing over his shoulder. 'All right, soak it up lads, but don't ask any questions. Religion, nothing. Ah've been here twenty years and ah've seen it all and ah don't want trouble. All right? In you go.'

We started by soaking up two pints of bitter, wedged into the lounge bar. It was humid and loud, English football playing on TV, old Rangers shirts and photos mounted around the walls. People were downing their drink, shouting conversation, three deep at the bar or tucked in alcoves. Three big men in leather jackets pushed past us to join an animated crowd smoking away in the far corner. It was serious – no smiling, no laughing – but not angry. You could, however, imagine what might happen were someone in green to walk in.

A little later we snagged two low stools and edged into a table where a couple of men were drinking moodily. They ignored us until Toby brought me a half-pint refill.

'Can't handle your drink?' the elder one said scathingly.

My glass did look puny. 'I'm just not thirsty.' The man looked deeply unimpressed. 'And I've got a flight to catch.' That was probably a mistake.

'Where?'

'London.'

A scowl. 'You live there?'

'No. Los Angeles. I always wanted to see the Old Firm. One of the great games.'

He nodded. 'Nothing else like it. That's a long way to come to get beat. How did you find a ticket?'

'A friend of mine in Los Angeles is a die-hard fanatic. He'll be in a bar now, watching it on TV. Just like this but four in the morning.'

'Wasted his time getting out of bed today.' He drank and wiped his mouth with his hand. 'So what did you think of it?'

I thought for a second. 'I think we controlled the game. Our build-up was slow but we were unlucky.'

The man snorted. 'We? Who's we?'

'Rangers, I mean. I'm not a die-hard but I know who I wanted to win.' It wasn't really true. There's precious little at an Old Firm game for the neutral to support on either side. I glanced at Toby to make sure his hooped shirt was hidden under his coat.

'Well I am a fuckin' die-hard and I couldnae get a ticket,' said the man thickly. 'You're verrah lucky.'

Based on the game we'd just suffered through I wasn't so sure but I nodded anyway. Toby and I both sipped our beers at exactly the same time, like a double act. 'Rangers' keeper made some good saves late on,' I tried, steering clear of the we-word.

The man almost spat. 'Gave away the first goal. Horrible. You didn't see that? I thought you were inside the game?'

'It was hard to see from where we were,' Toby explained. Just then his phone started playing 'Land of Hope and Glory'. 'Alec,' said Toby, grimacing. 'Hello. Yeah, I'm in a pub.' He stuck a finger in his other ear.

'Aah,' said the man. 'Now we could see very clearly.' He finished his pint, set it down precisely and signalled for another. 'On the television,' he added, with feeling.

'Two—nil,' said Toby. He screwed up his eyes with the effort of listening. 'I know. I got timed out. It's hopeless on that band-width.'

'What's he playing at?' asked the man.

'He's working,' I said.

'Re-install everything,' said Toby. 'I'll call you back.'

'Working? And you're from where?' the man asked him.

'From York.'

'From York?' the man echoed, as if this was even more unlikely than Los Angeles.

'Rangers are certainly missing Albertz,' I interjected, sensing problems. I'd read this in *Follow, Follow*, so it seemed a sound line of fan banter.

The man ignored me. Obviously my goalkeeper remark had destroyed any minimal credibility I might have had. 'How did you come here?' he wanted to know. 'From York?'

Unwisely Toby smiled. 'On the train.' The man's eyebrows suggested lingering suspicion and Toby carried on with additional disclosure well beyond his normal levels, laughing nervously. 'I was going potholing in the Lake District with my girlfriend this weekend and then my brother emailed about this.' He jerked his finger at me. Our appearance, our usage of scarce tickets, our venturing into this partisan bar – all his fault, said the finger.

The younger man arrived back at our table with fresh beers and said something Scottish.

'Ally McCoist is here,' the first man translated. 'In the toilet.'

'Wow,' I said.

'You know who Ally McCoist is?'

'Sure.' Thankfully I'd been reading the tabloids. McCoist was an ex-Rangers goal machine who'd just admitted to extra-marital shenanigans with a television celebrity called Patsy. I didn't feel any need to visit the great man in the urinals. Irritatingly, Toby and I did the synchronized drinking act again. I tried to break it by pausing on the way up but Toby did exactly the same thing, so we just looked like a pair of chumps. 'We need to get going pretty soon,' I said.

Again, this was greeted with doubtful astonishment. We stood up and fumbled with our coats. I made sure my red, white and blue Rangers scarf was prominent. We shook hands with the men. 'Good luck for the rest of the season,' I called, but the older one just shook his head. It was unclear if he didn't want my luck or simply doubted it would help.

On the street Danny was still guarding the door. 'How was it, lads?' he asked.

'Shame about the game,' I said. 'Great crowd in here, though.'

'You cannae take any chances.' He was still worrying. 'Journalists, I mean. Come in here, say one thing, then go away and write down something else.' He mimicked a notebook.

'Well, I'm not really a journalist,' I soothed. 'I just always wanted to see the Old Firm. That's all, no hidden agenda.'

'Aah well. It's certainly unique.' Danny sounded tired, like most locals pondering the bitter rivalry.

We thanked him and turned to go but at the last moment he stepped forward and reached for my throat. I was so startled that I froze. He touched my scarf and shook his head. 'Better take that off,' he said. 'You'll not want any trouble in the city.'

'You think there'll be trouble?' Despite the incessant warnings it seemed to me that things were surely cooling off now.

'Those who want it always find it,' Danny said. 'Always.'

Toby and I continued down the Paisley Road past grand stone buildings with signs saying 'Available'. It was still raining half-heartedly, under low skies. 'Noisy back there,' I said, feeling suddenly hoarse. 'But a normal pub, really. I wonder what it's like when they win?'

'Better,' said Toby.

We turned into a closed shopping centre but there was no way through to the river. I wondered about a taxi but there weren't any. 'The trouble with Celtic and Rangers is all this sourness has lost connection with anything real. The fans, I mean. All that fuck the Queen, fuck the Pope. It's the cover story but this isn't really about religion any more. A lot of them probably don't even believe in God. It's not an argument about anything.'

'The purest kind,' said Toby.

'Religion ought to be private anyway. Other people's gods are too inflammatory.'

Toby spotted a public convenience and disappeared urgently

inside, leaving me to watch cars rolling through dark puddles in the road. A man came across the road towards me, talking on his mobile. 'It doesn't get any worse than this, love. Why? Why? We lost. We lost to that two-bob scumbag scare of shite.' He glanced at me and I looked away.

'I didn't know you went potholing,' I said when Toby emerged. 'Isn't it dangerous?'

'Probably less than local derbies, apart from when we have to swim through tunnels.'

I'd promised our parents a full report on Toby's world. This craziness would not be part of it. 'And how does Alec reach you when you're under all that rock?'

'He can't. It's the one time I'm safe.'

'I didn't know you had a girlfriend either.' This nugget would definitely be in my report. It might even signal a seismic shift from work to women.

'Aah,' said Toby.

'So what's she like?' I tried to imagine a sexy young potholer: long-limbed, a strong grip, highly adventurous. Or then again, broken fingernails, covered in cobwebs, and wearing a hard hat with a dazzling lamp.

'Oh, pretty nice.'

We crossed the Clyde on a busy road bridge. There were no ships or sails below. Central Glasgow looked unadorned, unamused, unfrivolous. There was a blustery emptiness, mid-afternoon on a wet Sunday was dead-time here. 'D'you believe in God?' I asked.

'Didn't you just say religion should be private?'

'It was just a theory. Don't worry, I won't tell anyone.'

'Well, not particularly.'

'Opium for the people?'

'If you like.'

'So what does it all mean then? Life.'

'It doesn't have to mean anything. Life just happens.'

'Wouldn't God be a comfort, though?' Comfort. The word felt out of place as we trudged up Argyle Street, past a pub with a warm blast of muggy air at the door. 'Maybe one more pint, then?'

74

'Amen to that,' said Toby.

We went in and I fed coins into a massively complicated fruit machine without winning anything as far as I could tell. Toby brought over two glasses with foam slipping down the side. I took a long, slow drink, watching him through the beer glass. 'Maybe God's dead,' I said. 'Or just washed his hands of us and gone fishing. Left us to get on with it and screw it all up.'

'That's probably it,' said Toby.

'It's Joe Obvious I know, but isn't it a big irony that schemes promising everlasting peace and love are the biggest cause of trouble on this planet? If we all agreed about religion, d'you reckon we could get rid of the fighting? Theoretically?'

'No,' said Toby. 'Religion's only a label, like you were saying. Fighting's usually about money and culture.'

'You're probably right.' I flipped through the crudely drawn cartoons in *Follow, Follow*. One showed a couple of Celtic fans looking confused outside a brothel in Amsterdam, where Celtic had recently played. You could tell they were Celtic fans because they were tiny, their faces were covered with scabs, they had holes in their clothes and they were giving off a nasty unwashed odour. Faced with this horrific prospect, two idle whores were pretending that the brothel was closed for redecoration.

We collected our bags. At Central Station a couple of hooped shirts were running like drunken aeroplanes under the train bridge, their shouts garbled in the echoes. Fortunately there were no blue shirts nearby, not yet anyway. We stood in the concourse where the lights were just starting to come on. There was an impressive array of white noticeboards underneath a big sign saying 'Information'. We went to look for train times and found a Kafka-esque blank wall, an absence of information of any kind. Toby's phone went off yet again. He listened intently for a minute, shaking his head. 'Okay, I'm coming, I'm coming.'

The departures board didn't show any trains heading south of the border, just cancellations and Sunday delays. A loudspeaker voice boomed and cackled unintelligibly. 'Better start praying if you want to get home tonight,' I said, feeling smug that I was flying down south. Then we looked over at the platforms and saw the small sign saying 'King's Cross', a train with its doors all shut, a guard whistling. 'Hey,' I began, but Toby was already racing across the concourse into the fading twilight.

Home

When Billericay Town won the FA Vase in 1979 for an astonishing third time in four years, pounding Almondsbury Greenway by four goals to one, I was one of the few residents who did not go to Wembley. Sadly I was required to go to school on Saturdays for extra Latin, fencing and elocution. But I showed up for their triumphal open-top bus parade the next day, eager to jump on the bandwagon even at that late stage. The Vase might be for lower-echelon amateur sides, but Wembley was Wembley and we'd won the cup. The word 'Billericay' was even mentioned on *Grandstand*, Doug Young's hat-trick being the first at Wembley since Geoff Hurst in the 1966 World Cup final. As the double-decker inched along Blunts Wall Lane, the crowd broke into song:

> Singing aye aye ippy ippy aye
> Singing aye aye ippy ippy aye
> Singing aye aye ippy
> We come from Billericay
> Singing aye aye ippy ippy aye.

Heady stuff but to be honest, before the cup runs I'd hardly noticed that Billericay even had a team. Their tiny ground was only a quarter of a mile from our house and a few dozen cars would park along our street on match days, but I simply had no enthusiasm for my then home town. It was the embarrassing procession of lunatic Members of Parliament that Billericay kept electing, like Harvey 'Spanky' Proctor (gross indecency conviction involving a rent boy) and Teresa 'Cut off their Goolies' Gorman (anti-Europe, pro-castration). It was the late singer Ian Dury's innuendo about Billericay Dickie ('doing very well'). It was those idiotic jokes. (How many Essex girls does it take to make a chocolate chip cookie? Five, one to stir the mixture and four to peel the Smarties.) And there was nothing to do.

Billericay's big angle has always been escape from Billericay. We had a twee teashop called The Chantry which claimed to be where the Puritan Pilgrim Fathers planned their escape aboard the *Mayflower*, the town's symbol. For a bored teenager three hundred and fifty years later, escape was aboard the green 151 bus past Great Burstead and down Noak Hill to big bad Basildon. (What do you call an Essex girl with an IQ of 150? Basildon.) Basildon was Sodom and Gomorrah, relatively speaking, a New Town centred on a windswept concrete shopping precinct where my oldest friend Nigel and I practised loitering. It also had a swimming pool where we ogled Basildon's lost girls, and a cinema of the damned where we saw *Earthquake, Airport, The Poseidon Adventure, The Towering Inferno* and *Jaws*.

Billericay people looked down from our hilltop on Basildon. They sniffed at its resettled cockneys in council flats, all its vulgar newness. After we won the Vase I went to see Billericay's Isthmian League derby clash against Basildon. It was drizzling. I leaned against a railing behind one goal and watched Billericay's supporters in the main stand, essentially a very long garden shed, try to rile the Basildon manager's basset hound, which fell asleep tied to a dustbin.

I learned to ride a bicycle in Billericay. Stole plastic zebras from the toy shop. Practised ping-pong on a warped home-made table. Squashed pennies on the railway track. Made walnut fudge for my dad's birthday. Found my first job collecting money for a lazy window cleaner. Got thrown out of a pub. Joined the local old-biddies bridge club. Opened a bank account. Went overdrawn. Passed my driving test. Got thrown out of another pub. I grew up in Billericay. I just didn't want to come from Billericay.

Nigel and I rode a Milan tram out to the San Siro. What a stadium! It's an enormous square box with white round towers at each corner that look like monstrous spiralling barbers' poles twelve floors high. The place has a glass roof hung on long criss-cross girders, floating above the field and magnifying the crowd-roar beneath. Eighty thousand seats wrap around all four sides, climbing from the row right by the sidelines where we'd just sat down. The front row! Above the highest seats but below the roof the city skyline was twinkling through Milanese fog mixed with smoke flares from the hard-core ultras. Barely ten yards away Rui Costa and Maldini, stretching and flexing, were talking tactics. Vendors strolled past selling ice cream and coffee. The Curva Nord was a mass of medieval-looking Internazionale banners in blue and black – the *nerazzurri*. Opposite them hung AC Milan's red and black flags, draped over the Curva Sud's triple tiers – the *rossoneri*. It was a few minutes past eight-thirty. The world's most recognizable referee, bald sunken-eyed Collina, had his whistle poised. This was Serie A, as good as it gets, and the derby game of the year. This was Big.

For a while it had looked as if we'd miss the kick-off. The San Siro has numbered entrances around its maximum security perimeter fence. The first gate we saw was 24 and our tickets had 61 on them so we set off, wiggling through dense-packed queues at each gate. But bewilderment set in when the numbers stopped at 51. We started asking and everyone made theatrical circular gestures at us: back to the other side. That's when we spotted that the system operated not on numbers but colours, one for each side of the box.

Back on the *Arancio* (Orange) side we picked a line and inched forward as the minutes ticked down to kick-off. Gradually polite murmurs of discontent began to well-up at our slow progress toward the turnstile. 'Allora!' cried a man in front of us, echoed immediately down the line. Just then a trio of youths scampered up to the fence, just where it ran into one of the spiral staircases, taking matters into their own hands. One hoisted the second on to the third's back. From there the climber lunged for the top of the fence, swung precariously, then hauled himself astride, flipped sideways and disappeared into the stairwell. A cautious cheer went up from the watching crowd. Immediately a couple more break-and-enter merchants ran up and hoisted another gymnast.

'What do you think?' Nigel said. 'I could give you a bunk-up.'

'I don't know.' I could see myself dangling helplessly from the fence while the crowd jeered. I suspected that Nigel, well aware of my determination not to miss anything, was secretly relishing the same prospect. 'Why don't I give *you* a bunk-up?' I countered.

A third scrambled up, then a fourth. And that's when the riot cops charged in, grabbing the fifth climber and dragging him away. Of course, I could have done it. Easy.

It was almost eight-thirty when they told us we could ignore the colour coding and enter anywhere. We ran around to some gates without lines and trotted inside, coming out at pitch-level next to a row of fans in wheelchairs right behind advertising boards for Osama fountain pens, this being the style capital of the Western world. We walked along the touchline and found our seats, shocked that *fila 1* actually meant the front row.

This had only happened to me once before, at a concert in St Louis, Missouri. I was working as a consultant for the local phone company and happened to see an ad for Billy Idol, very much an Essex Man sort of pop star. With nothing planned I strolled over to the theatre after work, wearing a pin-striped suit. They had a few tickets left and I learned an important lesson when they offered me a choice between seventeen and nineteen dollars. Two bucks more is trivial. Pay up – you never know what might happen. In my case it meant front row centre, which at a Billy Idol concert meant being sandwiched between adoring biker guys holding out helmets for him to bless and adoring foxy chicks selected by Central Casting to make the video of the show look more appealing. I doubt they were able to use any of the footage that night, with this stiff guy in a navy suit, white shirt and red tie swaying to 'Rebel Yell' among the frenzied groupies, but I enjoyed myself. Mr Idol enjoyed himself too. Hobbling around the stage with a walking stick following a recent motorbike spill didn't stop him from having bizarre simulated sex with a thirty-foot inflatable woman or from confiding, with his sneery leer, that his two hot back-up singers weren't wearing any knickers because the tour couldn't afford them. Despite being in the very front row I was unable to confirm this.

At the San Siro, being in the front row was a mixed blessing. When the play was near us, we had the best seats in the house: beads of sweat, clumps of grass, thwack of ball. We were almost on stage and I constantly felt like an extra wide-man that Maldini might use for an outlet pass at any moment. On the other hand, when play was anywhere else it was impossible to tell what was going on. We had no elevation, no perspective. It was more like playing than spectating.

The players seemed oblivious to the fans, despite our closeness. But I suspect they're not. They remember as they make a break near the other team's penalty box: there's that gorgeous brunette again in a fur coat with her mouth open, smiling faintly — oops, lost the ball. They hear our abuse too. (Remember Eric Cantona's judo attack on a Crystal Palace supporter after one too many insults?) We fans, if we're doing our job at asserting home advantage, are tremendously distracting. Just ask Nigel.

It was actually my Greatest Ever Football Moment, even though we ultimately got hammered 5–1. I was left wing in our absurdly adventurous two-three-five formation on the junior school team, back in Billericay. We were playing cross-town rivals Buttsbury, on our patch, in our first ever competitive match. The whole school was dragged outside to provide support. I don't remember much, except being nervous because my mother was coming to watch, and discovering that our team shirts were gigantic woolly sacks that made us look like miniature druids. As we stood waiting for Mr McGoldrick to whistle for kick-off my teeth were chattering with cold and fear. Buttsbury looked bigger than us. They had played before. Mr McGoldrick had told us they were very dangerous and then he hadn't told us what on earth to do about it.

Things started badly and quickly got worse. We were getting overrun and the ball rarely came out to my appointed slot along the left wing. Nigel was in the crowd of a couple of hundred, huddled along my side. He started commenting on our disarray and since I had minimal footballing duties, we fell into conversation. After all, we were best friends, members of a trouble-stirring gang (of two) that we had named the Bumbry Boys — why, I've no idea.

Throw-in to Billericay. Mark Wilson, our captain, attempts to find someone to throw the ball to. Deep in conversation with Nigel, I must blend into the crowd since no one from Buttsbury bothers to cover me. Mark seizes his chance and lobs the ball my way. Taken off-guard, I catch it.

There's no catching in football, as most people know. I feel the skin-crawling horror of this moment just as badly today as I did back in 1972. The crowd falls silent. Mr McGoldrick blows his whistle. Mark Wilson gives me an appraising glance. Nigel says, loudly: 'Why did you do that?' Someone from Buttsbury takes the free-kick and I stand next to him watching the ball spiral towards our goal, feeling small and cold and stupid, and hoping that my mother isn't there yet.

And then, a football time-capsule. Billericay Junior School mounts a rare attack, up the right wing of course, since our team has given up passing to me. I amble along, vaguely parallel, when a team-mate hits a hopeful cross. I'm open as the ball comes towards me near the penalty box. I'm running. I control the ball with my left foot, one touch. I take it on a couple of strides. One of those big Buttsbury boys is closing in one me, I can feel him about to tackle. I'm half a step ahead, my shoulder holding him off, ten yards from goal, the keeper crouching. I shoot knee-high, my third touch, and the keeper dives but misses. The ball is past him, clean through the goal – no net – flying on and bouncing once, twice, and smacking into Mrs Howells' old pre-fab classroom where Nigel and I brawled with Jimmy Tyler and the other orphanage kids all last year. Goal. One-nil. I've scored for Billericay. I've damn well scored. People are cheering, and back down the sidelines I can see Nigel jumping into the air with his fists clenched as we all trot back to our half and Buttsbury's goalie slouches off to fetch the ball.

This may be the happiest moment of my life. Doesn't matter that I never touched the ball again. Doesn't matter that I was substituted at half-time, or that my mother was late and missed the whole thing. It certainly doesn't matter that we conceded five goals and lost. I got it right and scored. Tap, tap, bang. Years later I had to write essays explaining who I was for postgraduate study in

California. 'Tell us what made you who you are,' they demanded. I wrote a tear-jerker about this moment, how it forged my character and made me believe in the All-American virtue of opportunism, being in the right place at the right time. Total rubbish, but my lone goal was still weaving its magic fifteen years later and I was accepted. (And here I am, still bathing happily in the nostalgia, like Geoff Hurst and all that.) Tap, tap, bang.

Just like Billericay Junior School, Internazionale made a poor start to the Milan derby and then promptly scored. From our perch behind the wheelchairs it was hard to follow, but a weak cross escaped Milan's defence, someone hoiked it into the six-yard box and an Inter forward lunged to poke the ball over the line. In unison all the advertisements behind the goal promptly flipped from fountain pens to Lanson champagne.

The San Siro erupted and Nigel and I had the unusual luxury of being able not only to stand up, but run around in generous circles between *fila* 1 and the wheelchair folks, many of whom were spinning in happy circles too. I felt huge relief amid the mass ecstasy. With three 0–0 draws already on the Serie A docket that day, I'd been worried that we might have another Italian scoreless bore-draw on our hands. But with Inter's early goal, Milan would have to attack and my latest ocean-crossing would not have been to witness a snoozer.

The Curva Nord's relief was completely unrelated to my personal desire for grand spectacle. Last time these teams met, Milan had obliterated Inter 6–0. One of those days when everything went in and so the *rossoneri* had all sorts of banners reminding everyone of that remarkable scoreline. But for Inter, this goal put an end to a summer's shame. Only tonight mattered now – the slate was clean. Another teasing Milan flag said *Ronaldo, solo per Playstation*, yet the *nerazzurri* had gone ahead without their perpetually injured Brazilian superstar watching from the stands before he dumped them for Madrid.

One of the great things about a goal in Italy is that you get a firework display. Not rockets over the stadium, but fire directly among the crowd. At the Inter end a series of bonfires appeared near each exit tunnel, silhouetting the dancing hordes. Ultras balanced precariously on railings, high in the sky, waving smoke bombs. Firecrackers rattled like gunfire. Celebration, salvation, redemption: the party was beginning early.

Not that all eighty thousand were in agreement. Both Inter and Milan play their games at the San Siro, making postmodern mockery of the traditional concept of home field advantage. After that 6–0 massacre an Inter player couldn't wipe the mud from his nose and say 'Wait till we bring them back to our place and we'll give 'em a right tonking.' Tonight the San Siro was technically Inter's place, so they had the season tickets along each flank, although the colours looked mixed up. Only the two ends, the *curvas*, were controlled territory, Inter to the north and Milan opposite. No intimidation factor for either side, although right now, Inter's masses were making all the noise. They sounded like the raunchy anthems in a cheap recording of *Carmina Burana*, low and throaty, frayed at the edges.

Now I looked, I saw that Milan didn't hold the entire Curva Sud. The bottom deck was empty behind the goal as far back as the overhanging roof of the tier above, where the *rossoneri* were sitting in stunned silence. After a few minutes I realized what was going on. No Inter fans would be so foolhardy as to sit below Milan's maniacs up on the ledge. There was no telling what might land on them. The previous season, a brigade of Inter ultras had managed to smuggle a motorbike upstairs and had proceeded to set it alight and hurl it off the top-deck. If Milan's gangs decided to go one better, you didn't want to be underneath.

On the morning of the game, Nigel and I had made a pilgrimage to Milan's main train station. I engaged our taxi driver in conversation. 'I come, uh, Inter eh Milano, calcio match. San Siro?'

The driver spun around. 'Va San Siro?'

'Nein, nein. Not yet. Inter and Milan. Si?'

'Inglesi?'

'Yes, yes, Inglesi. Los Angeles. Who you want win? Inter uhr Milano?'

'The game, she is tonight. Not now. This night.'

'Le soir, si, I know. But who do you like? Milan? Inter?'

'Aah!' The driver grinned over his shoulder while running a red light. 'Cinque mesi fa l'Inter perdeva il derby sei a zero. Sembra che la squadra più organizzata, in questo momento, sia proprio quella nerazzurra. La nuova Inter di Hector Cuper è un blocco di cemento armato, un diamante perzioso. La nuova Inter ama attaccare e ama farlo con molti uomini . . . La grande Inter! Si?'★

'Block of cement?' echoed Nigel.

'Bit of a poet,' I explained as we jumped out.

The Stazione Centrale was a gigantic block of cement as big as the San Siro, built when Mussolini was making Italian trains run on time. The departure board offered an array of thrilling destinations: Roma, Venezia, Paris, Zürich, München, Budapest. We spent half an hour queuing behind old ladies booking round-the-world trips and finally bought a pair of day-returns to Lake Como, half an hour away.

The Bumbry Boys were as besotted with trains as with football. We had Hornby Dublo models, all the classics like *Britannia* and *Mallard*. We had archaic allegiances too. I was in the waning days of my early West Bromwich Albion phase along with the London, Midland and Scottish Railway. This meant Sir William Stanier, 4–6–2 Duchesses hauling crimson-lake coaches and Jeff Astle. Nigel supported Leeds United (nowadays he favours Millwall, maintaining a disturbing affinity for teams whose steel-eyed fans chant, correctly, 'No one likes us, we don't care') and the Great Western. This meant Isambard Kingdom Brunel, 4–6–0 Kings hauling the Cornish Riviera Express and Billy Bremner. Everything was a competition, from who had the fastest scheduled express to who had the wackiest goalie, John Osborne or Gary Sprake.

We excelled at getting each other into trouble. I persuaded Nigel

★ Five months ago at the derby, Inter lost 6–0! At the moment, it looks like the most organized team is the nerazzurri! The new Inter team coached by Hector Cuper is a block of cement, a precious diamond. The new Inter loves to attack and loves to do it with lots of men . . . The great Inter! Yes?

to make a series of reverse-charge phonecalls to tell friends' mothers that I was dead – killed in a car crash on Bellevue Road. On the other hand, I took the fall when we churned Billericay Cricket Club's freshly watered wickets into a motocross drag strip with our Chopper bicycles. But our favourite weekend excursion was trespassing on the London to Norwich main line. We discovered pre-1922 Great Eastern 'Trespassers Will Be Prosecuted' signs, rusting beneath gooseberry bushes. Armed with wrenches and hacksaws we prised them loose and smuggled them home to be lovingly restored. My parents still have a heap of this old iron in their garage and are always asking what I want them to do with it.

Nowadays Nigel spends weekends in his back garden building a live-steam model railway. No surprise, perhaps, that he spends his weeks sorting out Britain's modern, high-speed rail system. And why are most train companies financial wrecks? Perhaps they suffer from misplaced adolescent lust, run for decades by boys who viewed them as the ultimate Hornby layout. Football's just the same. Today's bankrupt clubs were run for just as long by boys who thought that they were playing the ultimate game of Subbuteo.

Who knows, maybe Ian Dury had it right when he sang about why trainspotters are besotted – 'We as trains are agreed that this is because we are extremely phallic.' I own a set of connoisseur videos showcasing famous British steam engines. Picture gently curving track and a distant *Flying Scotsman* pounding towards us, gradually filling the screen until it swirls past two minutes later, with sizzling pistons and whistles. Dozens of locos, hours of film, guilty pleasure. It's like nothing more than watching extraordinarily elongated pornography. Then again, my well-worn tape of *101 Goals* (perpetually set to Ronnie Radford's contribution for Hereford United) is like porn on fast-forward – bonk, bonk, bonk, bonk.

Nigel and I caught a slow and not particularly phallic train north through dull drizzle to the edge of the Alps. Wandering along Como's waterfront we bought a bag of hot chestnuts and looked at the boats. An elderly ferry was about to leave.

'Let's get it,' Nigel said.

'Why? Where to?'

'Wherever it's going.' The ferry hooted encouragingly, but it looked deserted and the rain was coming down harder now, pock-marking the lake's surface. A slow boat to nowhere on a wet Sunday a few hours before the Milan derby – it just felt wrong. But Nigel was already waving tickets and beckoning at the gangplank.

'These chestnuts are burnt,' I grumbled.

Surprisingly the ride was fun, an empty steamer out of season running just for us. The water was grey, mist drifting through the hills, as the boat criss-crossed the lake calling at wooden jetties with Italian flags. Each time a uniformed ticket-man would appear, catch the rope and help tie up while nobody got on or off.

Nigel looked over his shoulder and leaned towards me. 'I only got tickets a couple of stops.' He smiled mischievously. 'We're probably travelling illegally by now.'

I gestured around the empty cabin. 'What were you thinking? That we'd blend into the crowd?'

'We'll just say we didn't understand or we're lost.'

'We are lost. All I know is we'll be in Switzerland if we don't get off soon.'

'Actually I'm starving. Let's sneak out at the next stop.'

'It's either that or stow away in the lifeboats.'

Our ferry eased towards a picture-postcard village clustered on the hillside. Sneaking out was difficult since we were the only people waiting at the plank and the crew all called 'Ciao', but the uniformed ticket-man didn't care to see our tickets and we hurried around a corner and away. We might have escaped the long arm of nautical justice but we'd landed in a useless spot for lunch. The square was closed and boarded up.

I hoisted my umbrella. 'Now what?' This was more like old times: Bumbry Boys in a pickle. I looked at my watch: one twenty-eight already and no return ferry due here for hours.

'We can walk back towards Como,' suggested Nigel.

'On water? That'll be exciting.'

'There's a road along the lake-shore. I noticed it from the ferry. We'll find some food, a bus stop, we could even hitch. Shouldn't be a problem.'

According to my watch it was now one twenty-nine. 'We cannot, cannot miss this game.'

There was indeed a road. No cars passed, let alone buses, but it was picturesque, old stone villas with pink bougainvillea gone wild and Alfa Romeos parked behind peeling iron gates. These were places where you imagined a retired Milanese couple quietly inside, one engrossed in a novel perhaps, the other gazing out of the window at equally mysterious villas dotting the foothills across the lake. 'I must have this black cloud that follows me around,' I said as we trudged along. 'Every bloody football game I go to, it pisses down.'

Billericay had a lake too: Lake Meadows – a park with swings, nine-hole pitch and putt, and an artificial pond with a fleet of numbered boats for rent. Little kids could command tiny paddle steamers in a roped-off corner. These vessels were possibly the most inefficient method of moving through water yet devised. Swarms of four-year-olds re-enacting the Battle of Lepanto: rammings at two miles an hour, pinched fingers, the occasional tot dumped overboard into two feet of water. Graduation was to proper rowing boats with metal oars. I remember being wild with excitement at my first full hour rental on the lake, proudly pushing off from the jetty, away from worried parents, out to the open water and then a deflating sense of ennui at the limited possibilities of rowing a dinghy around a pond. Unless . . .

Nigel was Robinson Crusoe, so I must have been Man Friday. We landed on a tiny fenced-off island in the middle of the lake and tried to capture a duck. Intending to roast the wild fowl on bamboo spears borrowed from my dad's tomatoes, our chase was spotted by the boat attendant. Man Friday escaped but the attendant revoked Crusoe's rowing privileges for the rest of the summer. He didn't care. By then Nigel had discovered a Bunsen burner and a stash of lead. We built a Bumbry Boys club house in his back garden, hung a paraffin lamp from the ceiling, got the burner's flame adjusted to a low blue roar and began melting down the lead, trying to make counterfeit money that might fund a purchase of hydrochloric acid. We wanted to test which substances it could eat through: leaves, leather shoes, sisters. When all we managed to concoct were dull headaches we gave up and fell back on a heap of magazines we'd been filching from Martin's the newsagents, sneaking them back under our pullovers to lust over the centre spreads – Peter Lorimer blasting a free kick for Leeds in *Shoot* and an O-gauge rendition of Nuneaton Station in *Railway Modeller*.

In the distance came the whine of a car, changing up through its gears. Sure enough, a Mercedes swung into view and sped past, ignoring our hopeful thumbs. Silence returned, except for the steady patter of rain on leaves. 'When I was a management consultant we had a client deep in Kansas,' I said, wiping spray from my forehead. 'Specialty chemicals. Miles from any town, a complete pain to get to. We had code names for every client and this one was MFN. Slight crisis when they figured it out.'

'What did it mean?' said Nigel, teeing me up nicely.

'Middle of fucking nowhere.'

Eventually we reached another small sleepy village. The ferry jetty was closed but a timetable had good news: there would be a boat back to Como in an hour and a half. Even better, right behind us a white hotel was serving lunch in a comfortable glass conservatory. Sit anywhere, they told us as we shook out our umbrellas. We munched long crunchy breadsticks until our carafe of red arrived and then knocked that back until the spaghetti appeared. Contentment grew in direct proportion to wine consumption. The waiter knew how to serve grated parmesan: keep spooning it on until the bolognaise disappears, like heavy snowfall. 'I take it all back. I really could live here,' I said as the sun came between clouds, setting Lake Como on fire through the restless trees in the square.

'Eastbourne, I reckon,' Nigel was saying, when I emerged from my limp-brained gaze at the dazzling water. 'If I could sell-up and pack it all in, that's where I'd go.'

'Why?' I said, faintly disgusted at such an anaemic choice. After all, 'Sell-Up' is a fantasy role-playing game. Pick anywhere on the planet: pick Bora Bora, pick Cannes, pick Santa Fe – it doesn't much matter because it ain't gonna happen.

'It's near everything and it's got reasonable beaches.' Nigel's problem was that he was being run ragged by two charming but boisterous nippers who showed every intention of out-naughtying him, the 'world's greatest stirrer' according to a large wooden spoon Nigel once received as a Christmas gift from Santa. His little Tom and Laura were lovable scallywags out of the *Dandy* comic, capable of turning over an entire house in five minutes, expert at throwing a wobbly anywhere. Recently they had kept up a squirming, running, shouting battle all the way from Edinburgh to London, five hours on the train, destroying the entire concept of first class (Nigel's work-perk) for the other (paying) passengers.

We polished off some excellent lemon *gelato* and sipped cappuccino. Things were so exhausting back at home that Nigel occasionally scheduled end-of-day meetings in places like Swindon, just too late to catch a ride with the engine driver on the last train home, instead requiring a long bath, footie on the TV and room-service for one in a four-star hotel. Nigel had needed no convincing when I suggested a flying escape to Milan, my own fantasy sell-up. All he needed to do was bring back a handbag for his wife. 'About as silly as me asking Janet for a train,' Nigel grumbled. 'I mean, what gauge, what wheel-base, what livery, what fuel system?'

'Handbags don't have fuel systems,' I pointed out.

'All she said was blue. We'll just look in a couple of shops and say they were sold out.'

'I can't see you living in Eastbourne,' I said. 'What on earth would you do?'

'Plonk the children on the sand with buckets and fall asleep,' said Nigel as we ambled along the ferry jetty. 'That's all I want.'

Back in Milan we mooched around between downpours. We drank Guinness at the Osteria del Pallone, a football bar with framed front pages of *La Gazzetta dello Sport* from Italy's World Cup wins. Outside La Scala opera house there was a commotion and we sloshed across the square to investigate, expecting fat men but finding thin women instead. Under the awning was a real Formula 1 Ferrari, a TV commercial in the making. A kneeling man was sucking up individual rain drops from its gleaming red body with a water dropper while a trio of suspiciously beautiful girls looked cold and grumpy under long tailored coats – I suspected red bikinis beneath.

This frothy cocktail of sex, speed and opera perfectly fit my image of Milan. It's why, in my twenties, I decided that if I could live anywhere it wouldn't be Paris or San Francisco, but here. From where else could you get to lakes, the Alps and beaches all within two hours? Add the thrill of hanging out at the hub of the fashion industry, in a city full of amazing restaurants, a place with two top-notch football teams – it was compellingly glamorous. Loyalty be damned. Maybe I was an amateur from Billericay, but one day I'd transfer to Milan.

A friend of mine was sent there on business, acquired a wardrobe of sharp suits and silk ties and returned all smiles. Working late one evening, he'd been given a smouldering secretary to help him assemble some reports. Since neither could understand the other it was slow going until she beckoned him urgently into the board-room with its panoramic cityscape, unclasped his belt and hauled him by his new tie on to one end of the thirty-foot, polished ebony table. It took ten minutes to reach the top. Afterwards she ran for tissues and two espressos while he sat in the Presidente de Cartolina's red leather chair, faintly unnerved by the formal stares of a dozen predecessors hung around the walls. A goodnight kiss and nothing said the next morning – where else but Milan to be single, stylish and satisfied? As Nigel and I furled our brollies in the lobby of La Rinascente, Milan's famous department store, I threw him a derisive glance. This wasn't the sort of episode you could ever imagine happening in Eastbourne.

Sitting just off the stone-flagged Piazza del Duomo, La Rinascente is like Selfridges but with flair. We went up eight escalators without finding any handbags, let alone blue ones, then back down again. We looked at men's neckwear instead. A few years ago I had visited and bought a wicked silver model, top of the line. It was *molto, molto* lire, the down-payment on my transfer fee. Feeling too sexy, I wore it home on the plane. When I opened my little tub of coffee creamer it exploded – poof! – with the main globule landing on the tie. Furious wiping left a faint stain so I followed the advice of my table-sliding friend and soaked the problematic section in a salt-water solution. Success – the stain disappeared, but now the entire soaked area was a few shades paler. I soaked the other end but an inch in the middle got double-duty and now I had a ragged stripe. I soaked the whole thing for a week and the backing fell off. I threw it away. Perhaps my Milan was a state of mind, not anything I could actually possess.

We stumbled across the handbags on the ground floor, next to cosmetics. There were hundreds of them but not a single one in blue. When we wandered through the Vittorio Emanuele arcade past Prada, Armani and the rest, it was clearly not going to be Janet's day. Blue might be the rage in London and Billericay and Eastbourne, but Milan had moved on to red. Obviously Internazionale were in trouble.

During half time the San Siro flashed a Serie A league table with Inter on top, assuming that they would hold their one-goal lead. The red and black end whistled. As I sipped my *caffè borghetti* – small, sweet and alcoholically enhanced – it seemed an unwise tempting of the football fates. Remember Buttsbury. Yet whatever the result, I was relishing the purity of this Milanese rivalry. Here were two heavyweights – Inter with thirteen domestic titles and two European Cups, Milan with sixteen and five – going at it largely free of overtones. True, AC were originally a British club and when everyone else got fed up of being told how to play the game they formed the pointedly named Internazionale. More recently Silvio Berlusconi commercialized Milan and then rode a terrace chant – *Forza Milan* – into national government – *Forza Italia*. But the derby remains basic: no religion, no class, no politics, not even a side of town, just nerazzurri against rossoneri. Mix blue and red together and you get purple, as in our hotel's glossy guide book *Go! Milano* on the great rivalry. 'Uniforms even in politics form an atavistic hatred. But joined in mutual esteem. Like Peppone and Don Camillo. One not able to exist without the other.'

Back on the field a team of helpers was wheeling a giant pro-motional bottle of aspirin towards the sidelines and after my caffè borghetti I wondered if they had free samples to stop the trembling. But then Collina, a latter-day Nosferatu-Vampyr, blew his whistle and we were off again. When two coffee-charged Milan defenders upended opponents in the first few minutes, 'mutual esteem' seemed a touch wide of the mark. I liked 'atavistic hatred' better.

A quarter of an hour in, Milan found an equalizer. It was a simple, almost classical goal, slightly reminiscent of my own golden moment thirty years ago against Buttsbury when I slip-ped away from my marker and . . . sorry, did we already cover that? As a cross came in from the left wing, Milan's lethal striker Shevchenko fell a couple of steps behind his covering defender. The ball cleared the Inter player's leap but Sheva met it powerfully, heading down and back across goal, into the corner of the net. He rushed away to the corner flag, peeling off his rossoneri shirt and waving it over his head as firecrackers detonated around the Curva Sud.

'Those things can kill,' I shouted to Nigel. 'A few months ago some idiot lobbed one into the crowd and it blew up. One guy went into a coma and then died.'

'Where was this?'

'Another Italian derby, but down in Sicily.'

'Great. Thanks for telling me now.'

'You're welcome.'

Now we had a game, 1–1 and thirty minutes to play; anthems booming from both ends of the San Siro, Inter trying to regain composure, Milan pressing forward with new momentum. But if I was hoping for an epic, what I got instead was a massacre. Inter reverted to Billericay Junior School while Milan became the burly assassins of Buttsbury. Two minutes later Milan smashed in the go-ahead goal from a quick free kick, with Inter all point-ing fingers and hands on heads. A few minutes more and Milan got the insurance goal from another cross and header. And then, piling on the agony for the Curva Nord, Sheva slotted home an in-your-face fourth. Suddenly we were at a demolition, a dismantling, a dismemberment and the wheelchairs in front of us started rolling for the exits. When Inter managed a consolation goal deep in added time, it was the Milan fans who sent up a sarcastic cheer, most of the Inter faithful already hurrying for their scooters. Collina blew for full-time and we had our six-goal thriller, but now the revised Serie A table took away Inter's table-topping 'win'. Humble pie indeed.

We caught a Metro back to the Duomo square, gothic buttresses and spires dramatically lit, yet quiet as a church mouse. Unable to find the tiniest victory celebration anywhere, we turned into a modest café where the pizza was wafer-thin but so wide that it dangled not just off my plate but over the side of the table.

'The better team won,' Nigel needled, well aware of my rule about supporting the home side, even if 'home' had been a purely conceptual notion for tonight's affair.

'Do you ever get back to Billericay?' I asked him, changing the subject.

He shook his head. 'Whatever for?'

'Yeah, it's like that great song, what was it, "Deadheads and Cadillacs . . . you know. Don't ever look back . . ."' The waiter was looking pained. 'We were at the game,' I explained, as if that justified bursting into eighties rock.

He shook his head as he set down our Morettis. 'L'Inter è burro. My team.' Surprisingly, we had yet to meet anyone who admitted supporting AC Milan.

'I can't believe you like REO Speedwagon,' Nigel said.

'No, it was the Eagles, I think. Or one of them.'

'You've been in California too long.'

When I first moved there, he would send me tapes of 'proper' English music, like Genesis. 'Fifteen years,' I admitted. 'Inertia takes over. We know a few of the natives now, and how to go shopping without getting on a freeway, and there's the beach, shorts in January . . . LA's like an old shirt, convenient and comfy.'

'Hello! Can you say "Eastbourne?"'

Around twelve-thirty we hopped on a night tram which, like Inter, started fast and then got stuck. Our problem was the protruding wing-mirror of a parked BMW. I'm sure in most cities we'd have clouted it off without even stopping, but in Milan we pulled up an inch shy of impact and everyone descended to the cobbles to offer an opinion. After lengthy discussion, and a failed communal attempt to pick up the Beemer and move it two inches to the kerb, one strong man lay across the problem car's roof and held the mirror in its sprung-back position while the tram crept by at one mile an hour, followed by six trams that had piled up behind. Nigel and I clambered back aboard and set off, only to discover that our stop was two hundred yards further along in the gloom.

In my hotel room I tried the small-hours television and found three channels still critiquing the derby. No wonder there's no street life after big matches any more; it's all done for you on TV. Still feeling buzzed by the game, or perhaps it was the caffè borghetti, I decided to critique the critics. Each had suave analysts playing highlights forwards and back, forwards and back, in support of Important Points. Each channel also employed a pretty girl who smiled, chewed her lips, looked massively interested, but spoke only to announce imminent breaks for lengthy advertising, which turned out to be gratuitously and entertainingly sexist. After seeing all the goals many times over, I began channel hopping, skipping past two programmes still dissecting Juve's goalless draw from the previous night, before landing on a retarded variety show where busty beauties wore wet T-shirts imprinted with tonight's lottery numbers and exchanged wide-eyed hilarity with a nasty bald man who had a rasping voice and, apparently, tragi-comic bad eyesight. Enough.

The hotel's front-desk man next morning was miserable, yet another Inter fan. I caught the airport train wondering whether I still wanted to be from Milan: all that rain and fog, the relentless couture window-shopping. It would be hard to feel comfy and at home. The suburbs dragged on, an epidemic of graffiti on every wall. Worryingly, last night's pizza was beginning to disagree with me. At the airport, the young girl at Alitalia wanted to check-in my one bag.

'It is too heavy. It is the rule.'

'But there's nothing in it,' I argued. 'I only came for two days to see the game and my clothes all got wet.'

'Aah,' she said, dark-eyed and mournful. 'We lost.'

'Yes,' I said, 'we need Ronaldo back soon, don't we?'

'Very soon,' she agreed, tearing up my bag-check label. 'It's okay,' she said.

In the departure lounge I sat with a view of distant snowy peaks, sipping water and reading *La Gazzetta* to keep my mind off the pizza's exit plans. Milan's manager was basking in adulation for his clever half-time adjustments. The fans were happy. The prime minister had telephoned to say he was happy. The manager pronounced himself happy too. (Ten days later they fired him. Winning the derby ain't what it used to be.)

When we boarded the buses to our aeroplane, I found myself squashed next to a group of Americans. One of the men was explaining that he'd come over for the weekend just to see the game. 'What game?' another demanded.

'*The* game. Inter and Milan at soccer. It's like the Mets and the Yankees except it's way bigger than that. My son left home last year. Now he works for Inter. Dream house, dream girl, dream job. How 'bout that? Too bad we got ding-donged.'

As we took off I caught one last view of the city. I spotted the Duomo and the train station, but couldn't find the San Siro before we went through the clouds. I still had my fantasy of Milan intact, even if I'd never live there. It seemed to me now that the fantasy probably depended on *not* living there. The same for Nigel with Eastbourne. It really doesn't matter where you are now, simply spin a globe and close your eyes, because there's a wide world to dream about. Ian Dury may have invented Billericay Dickie but he wasn't a home-boy. Deep down he was black and blue too, an internationalist:

96

In the deserts of Sudan
And the gardens of Japan
From Milan to Yucatán
Every woman, every man.
Hit me with your rhythm stick,
Hit me, hit me . . .

The seat-belt sign went off. Was there a derby match in Yucatán, I wondered?

Eruptions

I pressed my nose against the window. As we flew south, the green mega-ranches at the bottom of California gave way abruptly to a patchwork of tiny subdivided fields. Family farms hungrily scratching out a living – no wonder south of the border they look enviously at Norte Americano mechanized might. Then the usual vastness of clouds and barren ground below, not much to see. No Yucatán, that's farther south, but any desert looks much the same from the air.

I'd drained my orange juice in one gulp, leaving a glass of aeroplane ice, so I sucked on a cube, feeling contemplative. I was visiting my wife's parents who were spending a year in Mexico City and they had promised to find tickets for *el Clásico*.

'You're taking them?' Claire had asked, incredulous.

'Of course,' I said. 'They'll enjoy it. And they speak Spanish.'

'They won't enjoy it the same way you'll enjoy it.' This from someone who spent the entire 1994 World Cup Final in Los Angeles hunting for ice-cream sellers.

'Oh, come on. We'll all be swept up in the passion. América against Guadalajara in the Azteca Stadium . . .'

Claire shook her head. 'I don't even understand what they're both doing down there.'

'Rocks,' I said. 'It's always rocks.'

My father-in-law met me at Arrivals. Gene had abandoned the whimsical ponytail he'd been sporting the last time I saw him, and now he reminded me of what Albert Einstein might have looked like, had he ever tried to slick back his hair. In the pick-up truck he chucked a report called 'Hydrology and Biology of Post-Paleozoic Carbonate Aquifers' on to the floor and handed me a fat book of maps.

'Page 127,' he said. 'We have to go approximately ten pages diagonally south west. I'm going to need assistance.'

I thumbed through the maze of roads. Most didn't seem to have names or numbers. 'I hope you've got a rough idea.'

'I have unproven hypotheses. But your trip is finally helping to "out" me.'

I threw him a glance as we wound out of the airport. 'It is?'

'Yep. I literally haven't been out alone before. All roads in Mexico City are insane, but I estimated eleven p.m. on a Friday night would be relatively calm. I'm not even sure if we're legal today. They have this thing called "Hoy No Circula": you can't drive on certain days depending on your licence plate, unless the ozone's over 240, which for all I know it might be, and then it's a "Doble Hoy No Circula".'

'Don't drive twice?' We bounced up a ramp and veered across a six-lane highway, swarmed by green VW Bugs with taxi lights.

'Get this. Anyone with a hologram number two sticker whose plates end in an even number can't drive on the first *doble* day and all subsequent odd-numbered days.'

'Look out! This bus is merging into us,' I called, flinching. Then a police car cut across our bow, lights flashing, disappearing down an exit.

'They love to pull us Yankees over. They grab your licence and it usually takes around a hundred bucks to get it back. Now I think the road bifurcates up here. Look for signs to Tlalpan. I can't see in the dark.'

'Tlalpan, yes. Bifurcate left immediately. Are you feeling all right?' Suddenly Gene was writhing and clutching at one leg as we spat out of an exit loop on to an even larger road. Stupidly I thought he might have been shot.

'Fine, fine,' he hissed. 'It's just cramp. I'm staying in second gear the entire time so it's no problem.'

'Right,' I said, gripping my armrest as we duelled with a Coca-Cola truck belching smoke. 'So all these rules, have they made things better?'

'Worse. Anyone with money simply went out and bought a second car for the days they can't drive. Everyone else went out and bought a wreck for the same reason, so there's more filthy cars than ever and nowhere to park. And the car makers and the big oil companies are secretly delighted. Typical Mexico City. Someone's making a killing, twenty million people living in chaos, and all surrounded by smoking volcanoes.'

'Makes a change from home,' I said.

Gene's home was the small town of DeKalb in the American heartland. Picture corn stretching away to the horizon, row after row after row. 'It's utterly flat,' Claire told me. We own a compilation of DeKalb garage rock bands, a CD we played just once. It's called *On a Clear Day You Can See Byron* – a nuclear power station fifty miles across the featureless Plains.

DeKalb is the place where some Yankee pioneer invented barbed wire, which tamed the Wild West, which created cow towns like Kansas and Dallas, which filled Chicago's blood thirsty meat-packing plants, which fed the country by railroad, which made America rich and self-sufficient and insular and uninterested in proper football. Thank you, DeKalb. Today's citizens cheer on 'the Barbs', the high school American football team, and there's actually a deadly serious museum paying homage to two thousand types of 'devil's rope' in all its evil glory. S-barbs, prickers, stickers and twisters – it could have been a *Monty Python* classic, except DeKalb did it first. (I'm *almost* certain that in Sycamore, next stop down the railroad track, the townsfolk – Sycamorons? – rushed to proclaim their city the World Capital of Sandpaper and put up their own gritty little museum to prove it.)

Barb City is also a college town where Gene is Professor of Geology. Since there is relatively little geology locally, once you've admired the flat 360-degree horizon dotted with water towers, he often scuttles down to Mexico to play with big rocks. He had something to do with that whole dinosaur – meteor – Yucatán thing, but I've never been able to get him to explain what exactly.

Eventually we exited to local roads and immediately got lost. Every few hundred yards were gigantic speed bumps like ocean waves. Over the first one I banged my head on the truck's roof and hunkered down. 'They're called *topés*,' Gene explained. 'They put them anyplace people need to join the road. It's the only way to slow traffic down enough to create a meaningful gap.'

We turned off and parked next to a four-storey cinder-block building. 'By the way, did you get the tickets?' I had been too preoccupied to ask until now. When I'd first emailed him that I hoped to visit for Mexico's traditional big football derby, he did some research at the university and sent back a typically sceptical warning:

An unnamed 'source' tells me that both teams are owned by the same group of investors and thus that the whole rivalry is hokey. You can either join in the journalistic conspiracy and hide that ugly rumour or engage in courageous investigative reporting and tell the world.

I felt he was missing the point, and knowing him, it was probably deliberate. Every football rivalry is 'hokey' at a trendy-lefty level – pure opium for the proles. But as long as the Azteca Stadium was rocking with fans who bought into the whole conceit of 'us' against 'them', who cared about the shareholdings?

We walked up three flights to the apartment and I could feel my heart pounding in the thin air. Mexico City is a mile and a half above sea level: how anyone plays football here I've no idea. The hallway smelled of spicy food and opera was playing behind the door. My mother-in-law, Jo-an, opened it wearing a poncho and kissed me on the cheek before producing three tickets. 'Behind the goal, like you wanted. And general admission, so we have to go early.'

'You done good,' I said, accepting a bottle of *negra* beer. We sat in the dark eating cheese and peanuts, looking out of the window at distant volcanoes, lit under a full moon.

'You want to climb one tomorrow?' asked Gene. 'Those little peaks are only ten thousand feet.'

A month before the game Jo-an had sent me a T-shirt. It had an image of Popocatépetl, the really big local volcano, erupting over Mexico City with a petrified child fleeing garish orange lava. On the back was some kind of public safety message in Spanish. 'Run away' seemed to be the gist. I realized immediately what Jo-an was doing. It was a coded warning: dangerous physical exertion likely. I made a mental resolution to start playing squash daily.

'It's bright out there,' I said, working on a second beer. The moon looked massive and hypnotic, like in a movie.

'It reminds me of years ago when Gene and I first met,' said Jo-an. She was leaning back in her rocker. 'There was an eclipse of the sun and Gene smoked some glass. We were just knocked out by it.'

I was bewildered. 'Smoked grass, you mean?'

'No, silly. Glass. To watch the eclipse through safely.'

'Oh.' I looked at my watch and it was one in the morning. 'I think I'm going to crash, especially if we're assaulting lofty peaks tomorrow.'

I lay on a pull-out futon, struggling to fall asleep. A life-size papier-mâché skeleton propped on Gene's equally unusual recumbent bicycle seemed to be glowing in the corner of the room. Somewhere nearby a dog was barking incessantly, at the moon perhaps. I was starting to realize that the lure of these distant derbies was, for me, a search for grass-roots authenticity. Local beer with its own odd taste. There's something unsettling about our neat, Americanized routines – marble-lobby office blocks, cloned shopping centres, Gap and Big Macs and Starbucks, fog-headed game shows on television – an edge of unease, as if we suspect that our living is bland and packaged and fake. It's hard to complain that much – after all, Starbucks makes a comforting cup of warm milk every time and it's right around the corner. (I'd just read that they opened a new branch of Starbucks in a Starbucks' lavatory, a joke I was trying to remember to tell Gene tomorrow.) But the process, and I suppose I mean globalization, has a relentless feel to it. How did I even know about Mexico's Verano league and América's special rivalry with Guadalajara? Because I spend weekends slumped in front of Fox Sports World, Mr Murdoch's splendid global soccer channel, that's how. I knew that América was stuck in tenth place in the Verano, equal on points with Guadalajara. I knew that both sides could still qualify for the play-offs. And I knew that it was all breathtakingly important or that it didn't matter beans, take your pick.

It was deep in the small hours when some kind soul finally went outside and put a bullet in the authentic barking dog. An hour or so of delicious quiet followed until a battalion of cock-a-doodle-doos cranked up shortly before dawn. I flipped over, pulled the pillow over my head and began to dream I was rolling over endless speed bumps as big as houses, hurtling down into the troughs between. 'Time to go,' said Gene, leaning over with a mug of cappuccino. It tasted terrific.

We packed bread, chocolate and bottled water for the climb. Jo-an, nursing a cold, wished us luck. 'Anything from Product Development yet?' I asked her. She shook her head. Jo-an had discovered that any sort of exertion in Mexico City, like volcano climbing, plays merry hell with your lungs. It's the thick choking smog. She liked riding her bicycle around the city but she didn't want to wear a mask like most people, because that would interfere with her singing. In true DeKalb spirit, she came up with an ingenious way to filter the air: little foam pellets stuffed into your nose that could be plucked out each evening, crusted in grime. Wearing nose plugs made you look funny, but let them laugh. She had sent an enthusiastic letter, before-and-after samples and precise measurements of the diameter of her nostrils to 3M, the entrepreneurial people who gave us Post-Its, but hadn't heard a word back. She lives in hope, but today, we'd be ascending Volcan Ajusco without nasal assistance.

We drove an hour and then parked the truck in a field. Ajusco had a cross on top. It didn't look that far off, and walking through the forest was easy enough, at least for the first hundred yards. Then came a sign that said *alpismo* and I realized that I would only be able to do this if I abandoned any thought of breezy conversation, kept my head down, took baby steps, breathed like a yoga-master and became one with the mountain. Above the tree-line the gradient stiffened to what seemed like forty-five degrees. Each step, on loose volcanic rubble, set off tiny avalanches. Suntan lotion stung my eyes. When I turned around to catch my breath, the vast city was all but invisible below the glare and haze. Feeling like a tiny speck inching across an infinite vortex I swigged water and carried on up.

Oddly enough, I have a soft spot for volcanoes. The soft spot comes from Mount Bromo, an angry volcano in Java that erupts every five years or so. High on Bromo, Claire and I spent the night in a dirt-cheap hotel near enough to the crater so that everything stank of sulphur. They rapped on our door at around four in the morning and we tottered down to breakfast where we discovered that we had one dollar and thirty cents between us, enough for a single boiled egg and two bits of toast. Then we set off across desolate sandy ground, a misty trail of a hundred or so shivering back packers. The eastern sky was just starting to lighten. Shadowy figures carrying lanterns trotted by on ponies. The stench grew worse and I postponed my secret plan of proposing eternal domestic bliss. After about an hour we reached a flight of wooden steps up to the crater's lip, where everyone sat on boulders with handkerchiefs pressed to faces, waiting for the sun, which in due course came up and we all dutifully took pictures. It wasn't as awe-inspiring as I'd hoped and the close proximity of skads of Japanese tourists with better cameras than mine and aluminium flasks of hot coffee made me too sour to manage my marriage proposal there either.

We climbed down and walked back across the lunar landscape while I felt jittery and annoyed, trying to gather courage and find some words. Come on, say it. Ten more steps, then say it. Three more breaths . . . In the end I blurted out: 'Hey, um, I was thinking we should get married, I think.' Horrible, horrible, horrible. Where was the bent knee, flowers, some bons mots about my so-unromantic-it's-almost-romantic choice of venue, a glittery rock in a Tiffany box for heaven's sake? But Claire said yes and we kissed (I remember her chapped lips) and then, surprisingly, the sulphur smell vanished. We commemorated the moment at our modern American wedding by having an exploding chocolate volcano cake with built-in fireworks, to the dismay of all nuptial traditionalists.

In a bit of a stupor I stopped to eat chocolate and watched as Gene squatted down, scraping white powder off rocks with a knife and putting it into a plastic bag and then putting that plastic bag inside another one. The scientific method. I asked him what he'd found and was rewarded with a short lecture that made no sense whatsoever. 'Isotopes, blah blah, oxygen sixteen seventeen, blah blah, deep core samples, porous karst, blah blah blah.'

'I see,' I said. 'This doesn't have anything to do with that meteor and the extinction of dinosaurs, does it?' Every day at home my three-year-old son, George, asked me why stegosaurus, his favourite dinosaur, had died out. Was it fighting with its tail, he asked hopefully.

'No, it's orthogonal. And the Chicxulub Impact Crater has been widely misinterpreted. Dinosaurs were already on the way out, based on small mammal population studies. The meteor merely sped things along.' He stood up and checked our altitude on his wristwatch GPS. 'Just over halfway there. Shall we?'

We reached the summit of Volcan Ajusco at noon. I leaned sweatily against the giant cross and pretended I was being crucified while Gene took my picture. Then it occurred to me that it was Easter Saturday and I felt sheepish, although there was no one else to see my sacrilege. Somewhere down among the smog, the Azteca Stadium was full right now, not with football fans but a hundred thousand Catholics singing that Jesus was risen. Way up here it was silent. A large bird soared on an updraught, floating up from below and passing overhead, its wings motionless.

'Tomorrow it's Águilas against Chivas,' I said. 'We're supporting the eagles, of course, not the goats.'

'Why?' asked Gene, reminding me of my son's relentless line of questioning.

'Because América stands for the capital, the mighty and powerful. They're like the New York Yankees: big money, always winning, a dynasty, city slickers, urban sophisticates.'

'Then I'd rather be a goat.' Gene was taking photos of rocks, including an official-looking hammer to show the scale. He once confessed that he wants a miniature replica hammer so he can fool fellow rock people with absurdly gigantic boulders during slide shows, the prankster.

'No, no,' I said. 'Guadalajara's like the provincials' best hope. Country bumpkins.'

'Hardly,' said Gene, loading film. 'Guadalajara's the capital of narcos, the true prop of the Mexican economy, thanks to US demand. Their cardinal was hit in the airport back around ninety-three. Assassinated. He arrived in a big limo so everyone knew he was either some big shot in the Catholic church or a drug kingpin. Or both! Anyway, conspiracy theories abound. Apparently a whole bunch of people jumped on a plane with automatic weapons shortly after and no one was ever nailed for it.'

'How did they get past security?' I demanded. The altitude was giving me a nagging headache.

'Your security isn't worth a tinker's fucking damn,' said Gene, surprising me by momentarily impersonating a hitman.

'Well, then,' I said, finishing off my water. 'God bless América. Plus they've got a pretty good Chilean striker called Iván Zamorano. It's a cool name.'

It took a couple of hours to descend, skidding and slipping all the way. We sat in a café and Gene ordered guava juice, which came in bottles labelled *Boing*. We drained them and ordered two more. A tiny child with long dark hair, maybe three or four, served us *quesadillas*, wiping down our metal table with a filthy rag that attracted a few hundred flies. Across the street, packs of kids were swinging in old tyres on ropes, squealing with glee. A truck growled past, dozens of people crowded in the back. Someone had left a sports newspaper on the next table and I reached over to take a look.

'The trouble with America,' Gene was saying, 'is that it's a safety valve for Mexico. Literally millions of exploited migrant workers have gone north. They buy fake documents, they make minimum wage, they get no benefits, and they're kicked out periodically by *la migra*. And they still send almost all their money back home to their families.'

I nodded. 'You know, when the US plays Mexico in Los

Angeles, it's like a home game for Mexico. Hey, apparently Maradona was just in town!'

'Who's Maradona?'

'You've never heard of him? A gifted but controversial Argentinian footballer. He's looking puffy and ridiculous these days. I think it says he flew from Cuba with a massive entourage on an official government helicopter to play golf, eat spaghetti and show up late for a TV special involving half-naked women like this one.' Gene and I checked her out. 'And look, he's got a big tattoo of Che Guevara on his arm.'

'Castro was just in town too,' said Gene. 'For a summit on global poverty. But Bush wouldn't show up as long as Fidel was going to be in the hall. Their motorcades crossed near the airport. Everyone said Mexico was being America's lackey for kicking him out. But while he was here, Castro said that only one dollar out of every hundred spent in the world goes to truly productive stuff.'

'He's probably right, but so what? That guava juice was probably in the bad ninety-nine per cent, but it was still delicious.'

'Cuba's health care used to be so good that Mexicans would fly there for operations.'

'Castro reminds me of Canute on the beach commanding the tide to stop.'

'So you think capitalism's got a future?' Gene asked, giving a boy a five peso coin to hold traffic while we backed on to the road.

'Do you think the eagle will beat the goat?' A special *Gran Clásico* section of the paper sponsored by Omnibus de Mexico didn't mince words: 'Collectiva e individualmente, América se ve mejor.'

'No,' said Gene. 'I'm serious.'

'Probably,' I shrugged. 'If only by default. The mighty market mechanism already won the big game. Now it's only got to beat Fidel and that Dip Shong Ill or whatever his name is in North Korea. It's like Churchill saying that democracy is a terrible system, just better than the alternatives.'

'I don't know,' Gene sighed. Already the traffic was glutinous. We pulled over between speed bumps and bought a bag of twenty oranges for a couple more coins. 'Mexico is a great country and it's got great people, but the government is fucked up.'

'That's true everywhere,' I said, entering the 'we're all toast' spirit of the conversation.

Gene plunged the truck back on to the road. 'A few years ago they had a fit of capitalism here and privatized the national train service. The Union Pacific railroad won the franchise. The Mexican President left office and almost immediately went to work for them and soon afterwards they scrapped all passenger trains. You want to go anywhere, try a bus. Of course, the roads are impenetrable.'

I peeled an orange and took a satisfying bite. 'And you're asking how that's progress?'

'Hell no!' said Gene. 'I gave up on progress years ago. I'd be happy if things just got worse more slowly.'

Back at the apartment I showered off a coating of volcano dust. It was tricky because the spray control offered either useless mist or water cannon. But malicious showers always make me smile. Some years ago I turned down the opportunity to invest in a Major Breakthrough in Showerhead Technology and I don't ever want to be proved wrong, like the people who wouldn't invest in young Bill Gates's geeky disk-operating system and now sob themselves to sleep every night.

I was just getting started in the business of backing businesses, along with my friend Wayne. It was slow going, mostly because we didn't have any money to actually back businesses with. Our plan was to talk to people with great businesses about huge sums of money while simultaneously talking to people with huge sums of money about great businesses. Trouble was, the great businesses that came our way were things like a sweat-shop that used illegal immigrants to re-upholster broken patio furniture, a new kind of steam engine, and someone with better-tasting false teeth glue. Jo-an's nose plugs would have been the pick of the bunch.

I remember how baking hot it was in Los Angeles that summer. I'd promised to take Wayne to see Colombia teach the Yanks a lesson in the World Cup. First we drove out to the shower breakthrough guy's house and I went into his bathroom, peeled off my sweaty clothes and had the best damn shower of my entire life.

The thing was programmable. It pulsed water, super-fast at first, then gradually slower and slower until it zapped you in zen-like quarter-second bursts, before bringing you back up to a final peak of wild, heavy-metal pounding. It was orgasmic. It got you in the zone. It was a better mousetrap.

But really, who cares? I'm with Castro. You can buy a perfectly functional showerhead for the price of two tickets to a dumb movie or a big bucket of deep-fried chicken. 'Better' gets a lot of lip-service but top-of-the-line decadence is wildly overrated as a business concept. Just fill my belly, make me laugh, hose me down. Fancy Colombia were streets better than the toiling Americans, but it didn't stop them getting beaten and poor 'own goal' Escobar getting shot dead outside a Medellín bar a couple of weeks later, drug cartel payback for all the money they'd lost betting on victory. We rejected the shower and moved on to a series of fast-paced training videos that taught cops how to defend themselves against a succession of knife-wielding petty criminals through the use of loaded guns. Finally we were getting somewhere.

Gene, Jo-an and I visited the Dolores Olmedo Museum. Dolores was a beautiful socialite who became a big collector of Mexican art. Late in life she opened up her brightly painted hacienda for public viewing. Outside the peacocks were all having sex on the lawns. Inside we found young Dolores – in charcoal, in oils, carved in wood – usually nude and always alluring. Diego Rivera, Mexico's most famous artist, did her from every angle, in between his duties as head of the national Communist party and looking after exiled Trotsky until that unfortunate incident with the ice-pick.

Uplifted by this dose of local culture, we piled into the truck for dinner at a quietly elegant restaurant. Strangely, there were more peacocks wandering the gardens. I had trouble figuring out the menu. 'What are gusanos de maguey?'

'Worms,' said Gene.

'Well, what about chicharrones?'

'Deep fried pork guts,' said Jo-an.

'Don't they have anything ordinary like that chicken in chocolate sauce?'

The senior waiter was charming, correcting Jo-an's Spanish and wanting to know why I was visiting. He had once played for the Vera Cruz B team. He loved England. 'Eeengland, si? Aah, Baahby Chaarrlton.' He held both hands out in front of him, offering us the vision. 'Baahby Moore. Gorrdon Baahnks. Muy, muy bien.'

'They played for England at the 1970 World Cup here,' I translated for my in-laws' benefit. 'Brazil won with Pelé. The final was at the Azteca.'

'Paul McCaarrtney,' said the waiter, finding a groove. 'Ringo Staarr. Los Beatles. Rex 'Arrison. Changing of the guard. You know?'

'Right,' I said. 'Good old England.'

'Los 'ooligans!' said the waiter, tutting sadly. 'So, what you do mañana?'

'We're going to see the Clásico.'

'Aah! Estadio Azteca. Enormo! One 'undred twenty thousands, all sitting, muy espectáculo. Very good, very good. And who you want?'

'América,' I said. 'Las Águilas.' A second waiter busy refilling our water rolled his eyes and walked away. The senior man winked at me.

'América very big, very strong, get what they want, you know?'

'Exactly the problem,' said Gene.

On Sunday morning we idled in a leafy square, eating chicken *tamales*, sipping coffee and browsing the papers. Gene was absorbed in an elaborate critique of the Castro flap and I discovered that Guadalajara hadn't scored a goal in the last two hundred and eighty-nine minutes. All was calm until Jo-an pointed out that my ears were an angry red after yesterday's heroic trek. It suddenly dawned on me that it was another bright, sunny day and that by sitting in the stadium all afternoon I would get completely fried. I never tan, I have English lobster-on-a-beach skin. So we began this weekend's inevitable wild goose chase, except today it wasn't for the world's best bar, or a handbag, or a place to eat. We needed a sombrero.

The stalls in the square sent us to the vegetable market, the market sent us to a convenience store and the convenience store was shut, this being Easter morning. Finally we raced back to the apartment where Jo-an fished out a cute white bonnet embroidered with lilacs. I stuffed it into my pocket and silently prayed for the rain that normally accompanied me to football matches.

We rode the *tren ligero* to the stadium, a green trolley that jousted with foolhardy cars at every no-barrier junction. As we climbed off and I first saw the Azteca, I realized how badly I had been underestimating this game and Mexican soccer in general. The stadium approach was alive: swarms of people clad in América's yellow and Guadalajara's white and red stripes, painted faces, stalls selling shirts, chickens grilling, horns *waah-waahing* incessantly, cops on horses. Looming up behind all this humanity was the Estadio Azteca itself, a curving concrete goliath that gave me a warm glow just to see it at last. As I jostled through the turnstiles, squashed in the crowd but comfortably six inches taller than almost everyone, the sky clouded over and rain began to spit down. If my hands hadn't been pinned to my sides, I'd have applauded.

After a token pat-down we found tunnel five. Over the years this has become just about my favourite moment at big games, twenty yards of dark and then that first impact of the stadium bursting over you as you emerge into noise, colour, bigness – and I'm just a spectator. What it's like for a player I can hardly imagine. It was an hour before kick-off but the largest stadium I've ever been in was almost full and the joint was jumping. As we hunted for three seats together, I noticed that although we were in a mainly yellow end, facing a steep cliff of white and red above the executive boxes opposite us, the fans were all happily mixed together. A giant screen under the wrap-around roof seemed to provide an explanation: *Todo Mexico unido por un fútbol sin violencia. El fútbol es familia.*

It was remarkably noisy. Mexican crowds famously bring long plastic trumpets and blow them randomly and enthusiastically. The effect was a bee-hive buzz, or better, a hornets' nest – a nagging, antagonizing drone that never stopped and every few minutes cranked higher under the echoing roof. The sun came back out and our end started a Mexican wave. I was delighted: English reserve, Irish luck, American ingenuity – and now, another cliché confirmed. But the Chivas fans were having none of it and our yellow wave broke helplessly every time it reached them. (Cue hornets.) Immediately below us wobbled a twelve feet tall inflatable bottle of Corona beer, guarded by three flag-waving babes in tight jeans. A goofy eagle mascot was winding up the crowd, leaping against the fence and saluting. A banner the width of the field read 'Guadalajara – soul and heart of the Mexicans' but I preferred an advertisement for 'doble fibra bimbo' – maybe the beer girls were samples.

In came América's flags and banners, paraded around the field while the home crowd sang the club song, which began 'Vamos América!' Gene had been looking pale since our arrival (he was worrying about the volcano Popocatépetl erupting, he told me later), but I asked him to help me with the words. 'It's lame,' he shouted.

'Doesn't matter.'

'All right. Let's go América. This afternoon. We must win. Let's go América. And so on.'

'Yep, that's pretty lame.' Salsa blared over the loudspeakers and a group of four enthusiastic boys and five thunder-thighed amazons gyrated out of sync near midfield. Oddly, this nine-some was called Six-Pack.

Men squeezed past with trays of Coronas. Suckered by the on-field advertising, I sank a cold one and felt pleasantly buzzed. 'Aah-gee-las, aah-gee-las,' the cry went up as the teams walked out to explosions and ticker tape and everyone stood, fists on hearts, while a girl in cowboy garb belted out the Mexican anthem, which has surprisingly many verses. Then long-haired Iván Zamorano slammed the ball down on the centre-spot and the one hundred and sixty-seventh Clásico began in a satisfying rush of yellow and white.

The play was fast and clever, often slightly too clever. The Chivas were setting the pace, all dinks and pushes, angles and nudges, threatening down their left channel. Country bumpkins or drug lords, today's opposition looked up for the challenge. 'Vamos América' called our end. This was just about the only song they had and they made full use of it. But although things were loud and excitable, I sensed an underpinning of friendliness here. Maybe Mexico, with its ancient civilization, is just an advanced society when it comes to politeness. Everyone we'd passed on the volcano had bidden us 'Buenos días' with a smile and nod. Or perhaps it had to do with the country's Catholic consensus, here on Easter Sunday. More cynically, Mexico is keen on football but they're not world-beaters, so maybe things just didn't matter quite so much. Or did my feeling of security come from things that were absent today: political links, religious affiliation, class war? None of the above, I decided. Most likely, it was just the inevitable result of sitting in the sun with a beer.

I had no inkling, but this game would be easily the most dramatic of any I saw and the reason, according to every Monday morning newspaper in Mexico, was Gilberto Alcalá. The referee, not the visiting team, turned out to be the real goat. Reasonably enough, he tried to let things flow between the boxes, but inside the area he became a stickler with the result that by the fifty-fifth minute we had seen four penalty kicks and the score was 2–1 to América. Each time the man in black pointed dramatically to the spot, tempers grew hotter. By the fourth attempt (missed! off the post!), the hundred thousand plus crowd, twenty-two players and both managers were nicely roiled up and the family friendly atmosphere had evaporated. A few minutes later a mass fight broke out in the centre circle and both keepers raced to join the shoving.

Moments afterwards, Guadalajara equalized from a high cross and header which left América's goalie playing dead on the six yard line, while his team-mates chased Gilberto around the field. Something wet sprayed down on us from the upper deck. The crowd was turning ugly. 'Culeras!' they bayed, pointing at the bouncing Chivas end. 'Coo-lair-ass.'

'What are they saying?' I hollered at Gene.

'I don't know,' he said. 'Wait.' He turned to a man on his far side and huddled in conversation, trying to hear over the din. Clarification took a while. Eventually he turned back with his report. 'It's rude.'

'Of course!' I said. 'It's always rude. What is it?'

'He didn't want to say,' said Gene. 'But it's anatomical.'

'Yes . . .'

'Well, I don't think he's right, so we can check the dictionary when we get back, but . . .'

'Yes . . .' América launched a chaotic attack that ended in a bicycle kick tipped around the post by the diving Chivas keeper. It was Roy of the Rovers stuff, end to end, yellow cards every-where, surely all someone needed to do was fall over in the box again.

'Cunt-eaters!' shouted Gene, so that a woman directly in front turned and grinned up at us, blushing.

'Thanks,' I said. 'That's really great.'

'Good grief,' said Jo-an as more fluids spattered down from above and the 'no violence please' notice flashed forlornly on the scoreboard again.

Ten minutes on and Guadalajara went ahead 3–2. For once the goal was uncontroversial, a simple header just beyond the goalkeeper's fingertips. Around the stadium, a fair sprinkling of white became visible among the swathes of yellow. América's recent hegemony over the narco-bumpkins was tottering, despite an increasingly frantic final period of home team pressure and heart-in-mouth breakouts by the visitors. Each of these was thwarted by desperate tackles and by the ninetieth minute I was amazed that our boys still had eleven on the field, even if the ref had booked seven of them. Jo-an wanted to know what the score was. Gene, caught up in the drama despite himself, demanded an explanation of offside when a terrific defence-splitting ball came to nothing and left Zamorano boiling.

Time for one last great attack. It seemed as if both teams had packed their teams into the penalty box below us for a crazy game of ricochet. The ball was worked out wide, cut back, laid off and someone was lining up a shot. I had time to stand up, then stand on my chair. The ball hit the post, possibly, bounced along the line – was it in? – hit a fallen defender's arm, I think – everyone screamed 'penal!' – bounced out to Iván, or someone, who crashed it back against the other upright – surely not – out again and hacked away. *Gol! Penal! Nada!* Gilberto bottled it, swallowed his whistle and waved away the protests. Final kick and down came more fluids. Another fight broke out by the players' inflatable tunnels, cameramen racing over, unused subs spoiling to get their jerseys dirty.

I felt structurally weak like a dunked biscuit. We spilled outside to the street, and immediately sensed trouble. A pack of youths came charging across us, chasing gloating Chivas fans, tripping over the tent ropes of a hotdog stand. Someone dropped down in front of me and grabbed a broken flagpole from the street. Others were lobbing bottles and rocks at the crush of people around the station entrance. Police sirens whooped in the distance. After all that mayhem on the field, was it any surprise that we were now getting *fútbol* con *violencia* out here?

Gene led us half a mile away to a pasta house where we drank wine until the crowds thinned. Across the street was a Pemex station where every pump had a team of attendants waving towels to attract cars to fill up.

'There must be twenty guys over there,' I marvelled.

'Pemex has a monopoly,' said Gene. 'Although there's rumours it could get privatized.'

'I can just see Shell coming in and adding twenty-four-hour automatic pumps and Slurpee machines.'

'Throwing a million towel men out of work in the name of efficiency,' Gene sniffed. 'All so I have to pump my own damn gas.'

In the lavatories people were wiping off their face paint, becoming normal again. I ran through my rendition of the offside rule with Zamorano as an overeager pepper pot. Gene topped up my glass and asked me how I'd liked the game.

'Terrific spectacle. Manic. A good game for the neutral, if you like morality plays. "Mighty América Takes Sucker Punch on Chin, Loses Cool,"' I said, unwittingly forecasting Monday's local papers. (Sixty-eight arrested, one cracked skull, we wuz robbed, hang the ref, and God bless the good old derby.)

Gene frowned and I sensed a professorial response welling up. 'I feel obliged to admit to having, uh, mixed feelings,' he began. 'I've never been in such a large crowd and apart from some inevitable claustrophobia, what struck me most was the frightening mob psychology.'

'Deep down we're all animals, you mean?'

'It was just like a witch burning,' Jo-an chipped in helpfully.

'I mean, you can see exactly how wars start, or religions – the incredible folly of most of the human race.'

'But maybe football's another of your safety valves,' I said.

'The near impossibility of governmental forces to act fairly or to protect people.' Never interrupt a professor in full flow. 'The incompetence and blindness and pettiness of ruling official-dom. The theatrical abuse and cheating of democratic processes. The culture of the gutter. The domination of gangs and extremist hero-worship, ultimately creating totalitarianism. And this over-whelming urge to rise up and explode, obliterating everything.'

'Like your mighty volcano Popo,' I said, twizzling spaghetti on my fork. 'I know. Isn't football great?'

The Edge

'There is nothing to match the intensity of this rivalry anywhere in sport.'

onefootball.com

I was excited at the prospect of seeing Galatasaray take on Fenerbahçe in Istanbul, the city where Europe gives way to Asia. Among derbies, this one may not be the biggest – in money terms, or international visibility – but for sheer fan-driven craziness it's hard to beat. The quality's good too, these days. Turkish football has come a long way over the last twenty years and Galatasaray, driven by irascible genius Gheorghe Hagi, won the UEFA Cup in 2000, the first ever triumph by a Turkish side. (Hagi was sent off for throwing a punch, of course.)

Excited, yes, but worried. All was not well in Turkey. Their economic crisis was worse than usual. Journalists had just been banned from parliament. And as I confirmed my hotel reservations, the Swissôtel was stormed by pro-Chechen gunmen protesting Russian aggression. I decided to stay somewhere else.

And then there were the fans. Gala's turbulent ultras have a long reputation for mixing things up, whipping out blades. Two Leeds United supporters were stabbed and killed before the UEFA semi-final. Gala fans refer to their infamous Ali Sami Yen stadium on the European side of Istanbul as 'Hell'. They drape huge banners that say in English 'Die For You' and you know they mean it. Across the Bosporus, Fener's equally hard-core fans have their own retaliatory slogan: 'Kill For You'. They mean it too.

In Istanbul, a dense, tense city of ten million that's part New York part Cairo, everyone's picked sides. Everyone's in Gala red and yellow or Fener blue and yellow (the one thing they agree on is yellow). And to quote one of my favourite sports clichés, you can cut the atmosphere with a knife.

I caught a red-eye from LA to Frankfurt on an elderly Teutonic 747 feeling anxious because I didn't yet have tickets for the game. The sports wires had been running stories about mad battles for tickets in Istanbul since this match looked likely to decide the championship. Although I'd promised myself not to go to far-flung matches unless I actually had a real ticket, it just wasn't possible. When I could get through on the phone to Meta, the manager at my new Istanbul hotel, he kept saying maybe but not delivering.

'We have been trying but it is very, very difficult. All tickets sold in six hours. Better watch on television.'

'But I'm coming specially to see the game.' Silence on the line. I imagined Meta holding the phone away from his ear and shaking his head.

The plane landed in grey Frankfurt at half past six in the morning. As I approached the ticket counters at exactly seven, Lufthansa's pilots went on strike. Blam. Woolly headed, I stood dumbly under the huge departure board as all those little black and white letters shivered and trembled. *Annuliert. Annuliert. Annuliert.* Excited TV crews filmed the growing throng watching them filming. Some CNN suit was rabbiting on about how this was the first strike ever in Lufthansa's forty-year history. A survey had discovered the pilots were underpaid, he said. Their aim was a thirty per cent rise, he said. My aim was to kill whoever did the survey. (I did feel pleased that I was getting so quickly into the gestalt of the Istanbul derby.)

After three hours queuing. I tried for an Air Turkey flight but was beaten back at the doorway. Traipsing back to the main terminal I got stuck in another huge queue. Gradually it dawned on me that I was behind an inbound plane from Istanbul. Customs took another hour as every bag was sniffed (by dogs) and opened (by customs officers). Everyone in front of me had packed carpets – another cliché that's a cliché precisely because it's true.

I spent the entire day becoming intimately acquainted with Frankfurt's airport: ticketing, departures, standing-by hopefully, trudging back to immigration yet again, gradually filling my passport with Frankfurt entry stamps as if there were a prize for the biggest collection. Finally I bought an Air Wombat hopper to Zurich and then on to Istanbul, dozing off in fading afternoon light.

Two hours later we descended over Istanbul's lights and the inky Bosporus – a ribbon of water dividing Asia from Europe, full of invisible oil tankers ploughing through the dark. At the airport I changed some dollars into a fat wad of 1.2 billion Turkish lira (billion!) and caught a taxi into town. The meter had so many zeros I spent the first half of the ride trying to get a grip on how fast I was burning money until realizing that we were barely up to fifty pence. There seemed to be thousands of small yellow cabs all swerving about like agitated wasps. My driver worshipped Galatasaray, repeatedly turning around and kissing his ring to demonstrate. People from his village had played for the team, he said, tears in his eyes.

There was a local English-language paper on the back seat. It had alarming news. The IMF was freezing its bail-out package until the government agreed to privatize Turk Telecom. 'Bloody bastards,' I muttered – this was what my ultra-Marxist Economics Professor Ajit Singh had always called the IMF. He kept disappearing to advise Tanzania for months on end, or perhaps just to escape from the gloom of Mrs Thatcher's iron rule. We students wore oh-so-clever sweatshirts that said 'What's Left of Cambridge Economics?' I'm sure Ajit had it right, but I've always had a contrarian soft-spot for the IMF bastards ever since, because thanks to them we didn't have to hand in any essays.

Now the military (uh-oh) had announced it was opposed to selling off Turk Telecom. 'Time running out for reforms,' warned a headline. But most alarmingly, finding tickets for Sunday's 'crucial' derby was proving impossible. Reporter Michael Severn had this advice:

Interest in the match is so intense that all over the country bars, hotels, restaurants and such like places which offer the DigiTurk (cable TV) service will be besieged. They will start to fill up hours before the seven pm kickoff and some will only admit people with reservations. Our advice is to get there early or have your friendly barman save a space for you.

Never mind being at the game, I wasn't even going to make it into a bar to watch on TV. Somehow I felt that the IMF was to blame.

At the hotel just off huge, chaotic Taksim Square, my fantasy image of two tickets nestling in an envelope, compliments of Meta, was quickly popped. 'No luck yet,' he said.

'It's not a question of luck,' I wanted to insist. 'It's just a question of money.' But that would have been too crass and American, so I left it at 'please keep trying' and went upstairs to find my friend Grafton. I hung rumpled clothing around my room and then we set off for dinner. Crossing the traffic in Taksim Square was an immediate adventure. The pedestrian lights showed a thirty-second countdown until they next turned green, indicating a possible societal issue with impatience.

Grafton is a film buff. He went to film school where he produced and directed a movie that is always almost having its rights sold or being re-cut for shadowy Hungarian investors. For a few years he worked in the library at AMPAS – the people who do the Oscars, and I would get free passes to preview screenings of Oscar-nominated films at the Academy. The strict rule was no talking or standing until the minor credits had finished crawling up the screen, even if they were in Polish. The mock-seriousness was superb.

Soon we were walking down a throbbing pedestrian street lined with kebab cafés, Gap, DKNY, Body Shop. Every now and then someone would greet us and tag along hopefully. 'Must be those "dumb money" signs we're wearing on our backs,' I said, spotting my first Galatasaray flag in an alleyway. We were, after all, in Gala territory, here on the European side of the Bosporus. Two dark-haired local girls in miniskirts strolled past and our hanger-on peeled off. 'I was expecting black shawls and veils,' I said, not entirely disappointed.

'There's a few,' Grafton said. He paused as we savoured the

basting aroma of a giant glistening thigh of doner kebab slowly turning in a café window. 'But it's an unpredictable place.'

'Let's go in here,' I said, salivating, but Grafton had spotted a menu just down a side alley. As we looked at it, a smart thin man wandered out of the restaurant door.

'This food is good,' he said, smiling. 'I should know, I manage here.'

Before we knew it we were clinking three beer glasses in a bar a few doors away. He recommended fish, always fish, fresh from the Black Sea. We were here for the football, we said. No, we didn't have tickets. Yes, we were looking. The manager made a call on his mobile, rapid chatter. He knew some people that might know how to get tickets. It was a club, very near, come, come. No, it wasn't a problem, he was off-duty and happy to help and the beers were on him, he insisted.

Before we knew it we were in a nightclub somewhere else. There was a twenty dollar cover charge for the show. It's okay, it's okay, waved the manager, meaning we should pay. The main room was dark and nearly empty. Two other men joined our table and a waiter brought over five new beers. Also twenty dollars. About the football, I began. One of the men jerked his thumb at the back of the room. Did we want girls? Now my eyes had adjusted to the dark I could see more people through a haze of cigarettes, women sitting on bar-stools with dark lips and painted eyes, no one smiling. No thanks, we wanted tickets, not girls. Sure, tickets later. We began to go round in circles: tickets, girls, money. I looked at Grafton. We have to leave now, he said. You must pay, they said. What for? I said. It was getting tense. We peeled off a few million lira and scarpered.

Twenty minutes later we were devouring fish gyros in a bright, busy café. 'I can't believe we fell for that,' I said as we relived our escape.

Grafton laughed with relief. 'There was even a warning in my guidebook.'

'It was the tickets. He found out what we wanted and used it on us.'

'Did you see *The Comfort of Strangers*?'

'No,' I said.

'Similar concept, except it was set in Venice. An unconvincing adaptation from the novel, I thought. What becomes of gullible visitors who get taken in by apparently generous strangers. It's one of the thirty classic plots.'

'What does become of them?'

'One is drugged and the other gets killed,' said Grafton.

'So our restaurant manager let us off lightly.'

'Alleged restaurant manager.'

'But you've got to admit he was right about this fish,' I said, licking my fingers.

Next morning we met for Turkish coffee in the lobby restaurant, where the manager was charm personified. I devoured an excellent croque monsieur, which helped strengthen my emerging notion that Istanbul was the ultimate Edge City. Everything smashed together here: West and East, ancient and modern, palace and slum, miniskirt and veil, Christian and Muslim.

The headline in the paper was challenging: 'Bilet Savaşı!' Underneath it said, '42 bin kişilik stadda oynanacak derbi için bilet bulamayan Fenerbahçeli ve Galatasaray taraftarlar isyan çıkardı!' 42 thousand . . . derby . . . tickets . . . Fener versus Gala . . .

'Maybe taraftarlar means "available",' said Grafton.

'It means no tickets,' said the manager, whisking away my plate as I put the last mouthful to my lips – what's rude in Paris is the essence of hospitality in Turkey. 'It's impossible.'

Next up, the Pera Palas Hotel, for more breakfast and perhaps a more aggressive concierge team. We took a vintage tram just like the ones in San Francisco and rattled down a quiet cobbled street in thin half-hearted sunshine. The Pera claims that Agatha Christie stayed there and certainly it was built as the destination hotel for swank Orient Express arrivals. The coffee was strong and you could choose four- or seven-minute boiled eggs. Gloria Gaynor was singing 'I Will Survive' which seemed terrifically inappropriate at first but gradually a brilliant choice of programming for the faded grandeur of the place.

'Fenerbahçe's ground is over on the Asian side,' I was telling Grafton. 'So it's Europe versus Asia, in a sense. Our problem is that they only seat thirty thousand but the club reckons they have twenty-five million fans around the country. They're traditional Turkey's team. Fener have won the league thirteen times which is great, except that Galatasaray have fourteen, including the last four on the trot. They're the new glamour boys.'

Grafton made a trip to the buffet and returned with a bowl of chocolate Rice Krispies.

'Speaking of glamour, I thought we could visit the old Sultans' Harem later.'

'Did you know, the last Sultan banned Turks from playing football when the clubs were first starting up,' I said. 'Claimed it was a pernicious Western vice.'

'I also want to see the Bazaar,' said Grafton, ignoring me. 'It's a superb location for on-foot chase scenes.'

'Could be a good place to get tickets.'

Grafton picked up his knife and sliced a piece of toast in half. 'Does everything we do have to involve this football match?'

'I'm sorry,' I said.

The concierge team were young, enthusiastic lads, split good-naturedly between Gala and Fener. Tickets were sold out, they said. Yes, but what about a ticket agency? They don't have any, we already called. Well, what about going to the stadium and, you know, walking about? Not a good idea. Many police. You would be arrested.

'Like *Midnight Express*,' Grafton said brightly. 'What a film . . .'

'Shh,' I said. I didn't care if we got incarcerated as long as we saw the match. The problem was, how would we spot a tout? How would we know what to say? How much would it cost?

'You come from Los Angeles just to see Galatasaray?' asked one of the guys, sporting a discreet red and yellow pin on his lapel. He wrinkled his nose, then reached for a Pera envelope. 'Okay, here is the stadium.' He drew an oval. 'This side is the VIP. Usually fifty million. This side is closed, you know, with a roof. *Kapalı bilet*, twenty million. And the two ends, open, *kale arkası*, six million.'

'That's what, about five dollars?' I said. Obviously all we had to do was throw greenbacks at this problem.

'I said usually,' said the Gala concierge. 'This game, tickets all the same. Maybe two hundred fifty million. If you find any.' That was sobering. But he hadn't finished. 'You saw the paper?' he said.

'Sort of.'

'Some tickets go on sale yesterday. Not many. So people get mad. One guy got shoot. In leg. People march in street. Protest about tickets. Galatasaray only got two thousand!' He sounded indignant, handing over the envelope. 'You watch in bar. Is best.' I can't have looked convinced because he ended with a shrug. 'But if you go. You support the Fenerbahçe. Safer.'

We shook hands and hurried out into the street. 'Did he say someone was shot?' Grafton looked genuinely alarmed.

'Only in the leg. Come on, we need to visit a cash machine,' I said.

We were near, so as a concession to Grafton we swung by the Kariye Muzesi, a small church built in the three hundreds. It was converted to a mosque four hundred odd years ago and these days it's a museum with some of the most breathtaking mosaics on its ceiling domes you'll ever see. I sat on a bench gazing up at Mary and Jesus sporting vast bronze diving bells, wondering how on earth we were going to buy tickets without getting shot or arrested or both. I've bought tickets from touts before and there's a certain way you do it, a slow shuffling walk, lots of looking around innocently, muttering 'Any tickets, mate?', not making eye-contact. Carrying this off here seemed improbable.

Our taxi driver drove like an arcade racing-game, thrusting in and out between other cars that are only there to test your twitch-abilities, which is what we were doing in the back. 'Me, Michael Schumacher,' he said, snorting with laughter. 'All taxis, Michael Schumacher. Crazy!'

'This is like a re-make of *The Italian Job*,' said Grafton.

'Crazy guy,' shouted the driver, gesturing at a lone jogger sweating uphill against the flood of traffic. We passed a police car that had stopped someone. 'Ha!' our driver spat. 'Police!' and he pounded a fist against his heart three times as we cut off a Mercedes. Grafton and I exchanged glances.

'Let's head over to the stadium,' I said. 'Get this over with. I can't do any more sights until we sort out the tickets.'

'Or go to jail,' said Grafton.

'Or get shot.'

Ferries cross the Bosporus every twenty minutes. Passage costs about fifty cents. They're big old wide boats – probably would go under in a minute if an oil tanker rammed one. We sat in the sun on the very civilized top deck and had more sludgy coffee, saturated with sugar to take the edge off. Minarets and domes cut through the skyline on all sides. The water glittered. The city roar faded. We slipped past the docks: rows of cranes like crabs on tiptoe and stacks of containers, the edge of a continent, no people.

'Did you know,' said Grafton, 'that George Lucas was inspired by cranes like those for the alien fighting machines in *The Empire Strikes Back*?'

'I think I'm starting to like Istanbul better,' I said.

'Last night won't be on my personal highlight reel.'

'Don't rule it out. Some of my most vivid memories are when I was afraid. It's probably the adrenalin.'

I sat on the deck sipping coffee, recalling a distant family holiday spent on a beach. Bored with sandcastles, I clambered up a sizeable cliff and got stuck near the top, unable to move up or down. A clump of stubby grass I was clinging to began to come away from the rock. I remember looking at the dirt packed under my fingernails and feeling my whole body clench and freeze. I glanced down at the rocks below and saw a cluster of anxious parents looking up, looking worried.

'Are you all right?' someone called.

'Fine, thanks,' I remember saying. I have no idea how I got down.

A little danger can be a seductive drug. I followed my cliffhanging by spending a summer playing on railway tracks. I found some builders' detonators and set them off by hitting them with a hammer, which flew twenty feet into the air. I skydived from a small plane along with a friend who broke his ankle upon landing. I went in the Scotland end at a match against England and fortunately the Scots won and dismantled the Wembley goalposts instead of me. I tried a walking safari in Zambia and stood twenty yards from a hungry lion, behind a trembling guide armed with a single-shot Boer War-vintage rifle. The lion stared us down, then loped off. I flew to Bogotá, Colombia and unsuccessfully pitched a wealthy financier to give me money to invest for him. We drove to his office in a limousine behind thick bulletproof glass that made everything outside seem huge. I found an active volcano and climbed it at night. Molten lava was dribbling down its side a few hundred yards from the path, a brilliant white-orange, glowing and oozing in the sweltering dark. A couple of years later the volcano erupted down the entire mountain, as it was bound to do eventually, burying the village I'd spent the night in, and everyone in it.

Vivid memories but stupid choices, to be honest. Yet looking back and weighing the memories against the apparent folly is just an exercise in second-guessing. What matters is how you felt at the time. For a danger-seeker, the answer is 'alive'. And most of these contrived, civilian dangers are really not so dangerous. The statistics on skydiving are very good. Lions usually run away. Financiers in Colombia get to work most mornings without being shot or kidnapped. The truly dangerous thing about danger is to find yourself needing an ever bigger hit to get the rush.

Stepping ashore in Asia was an anticlimax. There was just a sprawling bus station where it took us half an hour to buy a ticket and find the right bus to the stadium. Not knowing how to signal the bus to stop, we sailed some way past the ground, unmissable in blue and yellow. Walking back we didn't spot anyone who looked like a ticket scalper, but there were police around. It occurred to me that the cops might easily be running a sting by pretending to be touts.

'Funny, the one time we'd like to be pestered, no one's pestering us,' said Grafton.

'Wait till we put our dumb money signs up,' I said.

Behind a big iron fence, plenty of people were loitering in the car park near a club store selling replica shirts. The ticket windows were all shut. One had a handmade sign that included the word 'bilet' but it probably said 'Don't even think about wasting your time asking for tickets here, just go home now.' On the far side, next to a Burger King, some sort of disturbance was in progress and we approached cautiously to check it out. Normally I'd be happy to see the Home of the Whopper picketed by the League against Global Conformity and Cruddy Food, but today it seemed a low-profile place to stake out how the deals went down. We ordered fries and shakes and sat by the window. The police were arresting two men, patting them down against their car, going through their wallets, pushing them into the back seat. It was not an encouraging sight.

After the cops had driven off with siren blaring, edgy clusters of young men regrouped. I tracked one particular cluster sneaking behind some parked cars. When one car pulled away, exposing them, they immediately broke apart. It looked suitably furtive. It had to be tickets.

'Let's do it,' I said, feeling like Don Johnson in *Miami Vice*, but deciding not to date myself by mentioning this to Grafton. We walked very slowly back past the ticket windows. No one pestered us. In fact no one paid us any attention. We went into the club shop, came out, looked in the window, did another circle, went in again. Nothing. Back through the VIP parking area. There seemed to be more people here now. Then the cops drove back and the little huddles split up again. We carried on walking and found ourselves leaving through a side gate and walking towards a very smelly canal. 'We'll go to the end and then circle around,' I informed Grafton, who by now was clearly humouring me.

I've seen some rank canals in my time but this was one of the rankest. Stagnant and with a skin on top, it was nothing more than a rubbish dump for the flea market going on in the large parking area across the bridge. We crossed over, glad of a break from ticket trauma, curious to browse Istanbul bric-a-brac, bracing for being pestered once more. We never made it.

'Ticket?' said a man just after we'd passed him going the other way.

I turned round. 'What?' I said, looking for signs of secret police and not seeing any, which is of course just what you'd expect with genuine secret policemen.

'Ticket?' he said again. He seemed plausible, relaxed even, wearing a smart jacket and shirt. Which proved nothing.

'Yes,' I said, deciding not to beat about the bush. 'Tomorrow's game, right? Do you have two tickets?'

He smiled, opened his jacket and revealed a small stack of them. 'How much?'

'One hundred and twenty million lira.'

I'd lost the division function in my brain for the moment. I glanced at Grafton helplessly. From his pocket the man produced . . . a gun – no! – a pocket calculator, bashed in zeros and held it up for me to see. I was about to say 'for each ticket?' but stopped myself.

'In dollars, for two tickets,' I said. Now it was his turn to frown and look around for help. A scruffy old guy came up and I began to feel conspicuous. Some boys were poking at a large skip full of rubble just behind us. Were they in on it too? Our tout broke off from conversation with the scruffy guy.

'One hundred dollars.'

This was more like it. 'Are they good tickets?' Oh yes, very good. 'Are they together?' Actually no, but it didn't matter. 'But we want to sit together.' Laughter all around. No sitting at this game. The skip boys had joined the party by now. Time to open wallets, flush with our credit cards and scads of lira. We counted out five green twenties and the tickets were ours. They looked genuine enough. We shook hands, moved away. I realized I was trembling, but euphoric. Oh man, we did it. We got 'em.

'Can I see?' Grafton looked worried.

'Why? What's the matter?'

'Well, it's just this tiny date here. It's last month.'

He was right. Suddenly it was horribly clear what had happened. There had been a brief football strike a couple of months earlier, over TV-money of course, and a few games were postponed. Eventually the Istanbul derby had been pushed back to fit in the make-up matches. We'd re-booked our trip to arrive for the correct weekend but obviously these must be the old tickets – obsolete, useless, worthless. We'd been duped.

We raced back to the skanky canal in case the crook was still there. No wonder we hadn't had to pay top dollar. No wonder the scamster was plying his trade away from the stadium. No wonder he preyed upon people like us, dumb enough not to see the small print until it was too late. Surprisingly he was still there. Even more surprising, he seemed happy to see us. The date didn't matter, he said, screwing up his face and shrugging. That was just when they printed and distributed the tickets. It was Match 34, whatever day they felt like playing it on. Nothing to worry about. We decided to trust him. Then we went inside Fener's shop and showed the staff. Legit. When we told them how much we'd just paid they shrugged and smiled. We shrugged back. Shrugging seemed the right gesture for the whole thing. We went off to calm down over a beer but the waiter pointed at the police cars and said no, no booze anywhere near the stadium. We shrugged at him too, went two hundred yards down the street and discovered that the beer prohibition no longer applied. Istanbul was growing on me: given a 'no' you just went round the corner and kept trying until you got a 'yes'.

With thirty hours before kick-off, I was now prepared to soak up culture in earnest. We took the ferry back to Europe and refuelled on coffee at the sleepy two-platform station where the Orient Express used to glide to a halt, the end of the line. Then we took a boneshaker cab up a hill to see where the cruise-ship vacationers head during their two-hour port-calls: Istanbul's mon-ster mosques. We wandered around the Aya Sofia with slack jaws at the mosaics, the weird fusion of Christian over-daubed with Muslim, and minarets like intercontinental ballistic missiles. A crocodile of little schoolkids spotted us, chanted 'hallo, hallo', and giggling conspiratorially. From the giant circular dome an iron chandelier hung down hundreds of feet, forming a massive wagon wheel of candles suspended about ten feet off the ground. We climbed a series of wide ramps to visit the upper galleries. Expecting the usual spiral staircase I commented to Grafton on the novelty of ramps you could drive up in a small car. 'Not exactly novel,' he corrected me. 'It was finished in 537 and it was the greatest Christian edifice in the world until Mehmet the Conqueror showed up.'

In the Blue Mosque (shoes off, please), the floor was covered with a few thousand Turkish carpets, row after row laid out so that the pattern repeated to infinity. Blue Mosque, red carpets: were they hedging their bets for tomorrow? I didn't ask, this seemed the one place in Istanbul where Fener–Gala fervour stayed outside.

'I'm amazed they could build an unsupported dome that big in five whatever it was,' I said as we wandered through the edge of the Bazaar a little later, a labyrinth of utensils, antique carpets and spices. 'Given the technology of the day.'

'Actually it collapsed eleven years later,' said Grafton. 'Earthquake.'

'How do you know all this stuff?'

'The same way I know anything. Saw it in a screenplay.'

No visitor to Istanbul should miss a Turkish bath. We changed in a private sitting room with comfortable couches and emerged clad in scratchy towels. The attendants were loafing around watching football on TV. I donned wooden clogs and clomped after Grafton into the main room, another big dome in plain grey stone, warm and humid. I lay on a marble surface in the middle, gazing up through steam, beginning to soften up. The dome itself was cut with small star-shaped holes. Through them I could see the sky outside and beams of light pouring in, making jagged sunbeams. It was peaceful and contemplative, with just the background sounds of dripping water and babbling fountains. I watched dust-flecked sunbeams, felt my muscles loosening, gave myself up to the cleansing serenity, and let my mind soar free to greater thoughts . . .

In the long run, I wondered, should you buy shares in Manchester United Football Club? Or, if you can't stand all that success and moaning, one of dozens of other football clubs that nowadays have publicly traded stock. Although, to be honest, the crass commercialism that Man Yoo haters point to is probably the very reason it's the best stock to own in its sector. England manager Sven-Goran Eriksson said that Manchester United was like a self-playing piano. Old Rupe Murdoch, who already owned Sky, Fox, lots of newspapers and the Los Angeles Dodgers, tried to buy the Red Devils for a billion dollars. Now for him, the synergy was in the programming for his media empire. For your average punter, it's hard to justify a soccer club as a place for your nest egg.

An attendant tipped a bucket of water over me, by way of introduction. We agreed that Fenerbahçe were the greatest team in the known universe and he proceeded to massage me limb by limb, while I gazed vacantly at the sunbeams.

Most football clubs don't make any money. It didn't used to be the point, but when everyone decided football was after all a business, the one great strategic plan – buy your way to success – meant everyone lost even more money than before. The players started to wise up that their star-power was putting bums in stadium seats (and more importantly in TV armchairs), and salaries went through the roof. Success comes only to a few giants – Real Madrid, Manchester United and Bayern Munich win just about all the silverware, and a second echelon of biggish clubs scoop up the rest. No one else ever wins anything. My dad's first love, West Bromwich Albion, beat Everton in the FA Cup Final of 1968: 1–0, Jeff Astle. Dad fell on the floor when the ball went in and I was frightened there was something wrong with him. Since that ever more distant day, for fans of the Baggies not a sausage. They live in hope but, frankly, it ain't going to happen. And when your club does finally win some modest bauble or (like West Brom) gets promoted to take on the big boys, all that happens is that your best players demand pay rises, you build a mighty new stand, and next year you lose every game and go back down the toilet.

So forget about all that lovely TV money, football is a nasty business. Way too much risk (stroppy player quits, blind ref misses obvious penalty, goalie breaks leg, crowd invades pitch, stadium burns down, drunk captain crashes Ferrari into mute mother of seven). Too much competition. Too many rival claims on entertainment spending. Whatever you do, don't buy stock in West Brom, unless, well, unless you're a die-hard Baggy and you're doing it as a demented show of love. Yes, you already bought the new replica strip and yes, you have a pricey season ticket, but you feel a burning need to pay again and go all the way. Membership. Brand loyalty. Die for you. It's a small step really.

It was at this point that what always happens in the dodgy world of massage happened. I was lying there soapily, thoroughly softened up (I'd just been walked on), when my attendant asked if I wanted the special extra service. He wasn't a gorgeous Swedish blonde, either. I sat up quickly. And what, uh, would that be? Foot massage, very strong, very good, special brush made of horses' tails, more hot soapy water, just five dollars, give it direct to me after, don't tell anyone else, fold in your palm, like so, very strong, very good, you'll see. I sank back on my slab under the sunbeams. Of course, of course . . .

'Did you get the extra?' Grafton said as we sipped strong chai in tiny glasses afterwards in our cubicle.

'Yeah,' I nodded.

'Me too.'

There was a pause. 'No way am I walking back to the hotel. My foot's on fire.'

'Me neither.'

'Risk another taxi?'

'Sure.'

We finished our teas, stepped out of our clogs, gave our Masonic five-dollar secret handshakes and left them all watching the evening news: angry demonstrators marching in the streets of Istanbul. People protesting about the IMF or the banning of journalists in parliament? Nope, people without tickets.

With the whole city to choose from, out of curiosity we dined on the top floor of the Swissôtel, scene of the recent Chechen takeover.

Unfortunately they'd already cleaned up the broken glass. We were the only customers and about twenty waiters buzzed around us: a seat-pushing waiter, a napkin-flicking waiter, a water-pouring waiter, a menu-proffering waiter, a bread-basket waiter, a decorative-plate-removal waiter, a senior director of waiters to enquire about the waitering so far. (Très, très bien.) Our panorama of the Bosporus was dramatic, minarets aglow in the velvet distance. As a bonus, we also looked over Besiktas's floodlit stadium, the city's third big football team. Inside we suffered through a sustained but farcical attempt at pretension, perhaps because people who stay at the Istanbul Swissôtel want to pretend they're really in Paris. In any case, somewhere among the clashing cultures, the food got lost. Our waiters did that old party trick of removing the silver domes simultaneously from each plate, which was cool, but unfortunately so was the fish underneath – raw actually. The whole meal served us right for making the 'safe' choice. Outside Besiktas were doing much better: they won 2–0. It was a nothing match, but the stadium looked full and on the hills above hundreds more fans clustered for a free view.

Does fan fervour get more intense the poorer a city is? I think so. Football matters more to the poor. In booming Barcelona, the players are Catalan heroes but people go home to comfortable apartments and well-paid jobs even when their idols lose. It softens the blow. Here in Edge City, in a country trying desperately to climb into the EU/bastard IMF rich boys club, most people live near the breadline. One of our taxi drivers pretended to add a zero to the meter because the twenty pence we were about to give him wasn't going to make ends meet. When you're on the edge, it's easy to cultivate deep fanaticism about your football team. What else have you got to fall back on?

When I first lived in Los Angeles, I used to play football in parks at the weekend. Since the regulars were almost all immigrants, legal and illegal, public space for soccer in Los Angeles has no voting lobby and is therefore awful. Dusty rock-strewn patches, trash-can goalposts, wedged between empty public tennis courts and fancy baseball diamonds with floodlights. But they're packed all day and every day, with never-ending games of soccer. After a while my little gang of Sunday morning players congealed into a team – the Hollywood Cosmos, we called ourselves. Among our group we had three French rock 'n' rollers, a pacy German forward known as 'Scheisse' because that's what he always said when he missed, a sulking Peruvian called Alberto who had to be cajoled each week to hand over his one dollar contribution for the ref, a chirpy male-model cockney, and a clique of earnest gay Americans from West Hollywood who ran warm-up laps before each game and wore proper kit. Cosmopolitan for sure, we were also very much the misfits and outcasts that America is supposed to be famous for welcoming.

We played in the Los Angeles Municipal League, sixth division. It turned out that there were hundreds of marginal teams like us, most of them Hispanic, and all proudly sporting made-up shirts and talking tactics in all the tongues of the world. We Cosmos let our gay contingent pick our colours and ended up in bright purple. Things started well enough but soon there was trouble. An Israeli side, middle aged but amazingly fit, got into terrible internal squabbles and disintegrated into its own punch-up. Forfeit to us. The next week, we were losing to a tough Mexican team until Scheisse poked a late equalizer and then won a doubtful penalty kick. The Mexicans went berserk, chasing the referee off the field and all the way to his car on the street. Forfeit. Next up, the Orange County police team, who proved the old adage that criminals and policemen share genetic make-up. These big white lads barged and hacked their way around the field. I was flung to the ground by one thug of a stopper, who laughed over me like a replay of the Rodney King beating. I'd invited my friend John to rejoin our team (last time he played he'd broken his clavicle when I tackled him on to concrete-hard mud) and now he came to my rescue, haranguing the rogue cop, *mano a mano*. Two minutes later, with play at the other end of the field, the cop ran at John from behind and took him out cold. We gathered two of his teeth from the dirt and he ended up in the emergency ward that evening, getting X-rays on his skull.

The chemistry was collapsing within the Cosmos too. The gays sulked. The male model started picking the side and tensions rose about who was left on the bench. Alberto refused to fork out his dollar. The French goalie stormed off, tearing bandanna from flowing locks, never to return. 'I cannot do zees any more' were his parting words.

And I quit too. It was all too dangerous, too crazy. People with no money, no job, no prospects, no status, coming together on the soccer dust-bowl on Sunday morning, under a relentless sun, one chance to show the world you were someone. No wonder there were so many fights – it was far too important. Walking through the warm Istanbul night I smiled at the memory. A yellow taxi sped past with a red Galatasaray flag flapping at its aerial. Die for you.

Match day started with a bang. We woke to heavy rain and decided to grab a taxi down to the harbour. 'Be careful,' warned our concierge. He was wearing a Galatasaray badge: our deadly enemy for the day.

'Good luck,' I waved.

Our driver, resplendent in Fenerbahçe blue and yellow, decided to take the scenic route and we were still too groggy to argue. Halfway down a long hill, a car was parked at the side of the road. For once there was no traffic, but instead of simply pulling out and passing, this morning's Michael Schumacher completely lost control of his vehicle. It was a slow-motion crash, just like in the movies. First the parked car was in the background, then we were aware of it, then we realized we were going to hit it reasonably fast, and then we were scrunching up in the poky back seat (there were no seat belts), bracing ourselves . . .

Isn't your life supposed to flash before your eyes? All that ever happens to me is that my mind goes glassy and blank. On safari, when the lion looked up and opened its mouth (in what turned out to be a yawn, not a roar), I didn't scream or make peace with anyone or promise to devote myself to good works. I certainly didn't cleverly remember that all I had to do was run faster than one other person in our safari group. When it was my turn to parachute out of the rickety aeroplane, the last thing they shouted was to smile at the camera on the wing as I jumped. But there I am looking straight down at fields far below. In one ear and out the other. My brain seems to decide that despite all those good statistics about modest risk I'm just about to become an unlucky exception and it responds with helpless and cartoon-ish 'Uh-oh'.

We hit the car – impact – a short metallic crunch. We stopped dead and the parked car bounced forward, like one of those Newtonian ball-bearing executive toys: action and reaction, equal and opposite. Grafton and I looked at each other – shaken but OK. The driver seemed to have survived too. That's when we noticed that the vehicle we'd just gratuitously rammed was a police car with a red and yellow Gala sticker on the rear window.

The two cops were hopping mad. They actually hopped in place while shouting at the poor cabbie, who was beginning to realize the enormity of what he'd just done. Both cars were goners. His job was probably the same. Fines, jail? Another taxi was approaching and we flagged it down. Our original driver flipped off his meter with a shrug of futility, and his last ever tenpence fare blipped away.

When we arrived at the stadium it was barely two in the afternoon. The game didn't kick off until seven but everyone warned us to get there ridiculously early. We soon found out why. Police pointed at a queue that disappeared around the corner and we followed it along the main road with a sinking feeling. Half a mile or so later we reached the back. We were the only people in line not wearing blue and yellow, so I bought a scarf as a gesture of solidarity. Then we stood on the exact same paving stone for fifteen minutes until I felt compelled to walk back along the line counting bodies. I figured there were around ten thousand people ahead of us. There appeared to be a single entrance to our section, one of the cheap ends behind a goal. Since they were frisking everyone, I guessed three seconds per person to get in, twenty a minute. That would mean, hang on, eight hours in line. Impossible. But still we weren't moving.

'At least at Disneyland, they make the line weave around fake corners so you keep thinking you're almost at the front,' Grafton complained.

'Universal Studios' queues are pretty good too,' I said.

'I once got stuck southbound on a French autoroute on July 14th.'

'I queued for Duran Duran tickets. For my sister,' I added quickly.

'The *Star Wars* premier was bad. The line, I mean.'

'That play by Samuel Beckett about two men in trashcans. Or maybe it was Pinter.'

'You had to queue for Beckett?'

'It was a play *about* waiting,' I said. 'Metaphorical. Build-up of tension, anticipation. But nothing ever happened.'

'Like soccer?' said Grafton mischievously.

It began to rain again, first merely hard, and then a truly drenching pelting downpour. There wasn't anything to do apart from get wet since, as usual, we hadn't brought coats. We tried taking turns to stand under the lip of buildings, but soon both of us were soaked to the socks. Someone came along with Fener caps and we bought a couple, but they were a pitiful defence against the deluge. Staring at my feet half-submerged in a puddle, water running down my neck, I told Grafton that if Fener didn't have good drainage there was a decent chance that the game would be called off. I looked at all the real loyal fans, forced to stand out here for hours on end because someone didn't think it worth installing more than one turnstile, and decided that if the game was postponed I'd stay too, however long it was until they found a new date. Grafton wished me luck.

A little while later someone else passed our part of the line (which was still, frustratingly, the back) with clear plastic bin bags emblazoned with Fener's colours and Tel-Sim, their main sponsor. I bought two, peeled mine open and waited to see which one of us would make the horse/stable door observation first. The sky remained black. It rained and rained and rained.

That morning we had taken a cruise up the Bosporus. The boat

139

sails under two vast suspension bridges that connect European and Asian Turkey, but by now I'd abandoned my fantasy that the Gala–Fener rivalry was in any sense intercontinental. On the contrary, it was entirely local, Montagues versus Capulets, reds versus blues. It didn't matter to the world who won this match. But for these drenched young men in yellow and blue, waiting in the longest queue since the Tutankhamun exhibition just to get into their club's stadium, obviously it mattered more than anything. As a chant went up somewhere down the line and everyone crowded forward to see what was going on, I felt a shiver that was probably just rain, but which felt like the best kind of edgy anticipation.

Time passed slowly, fifteen minutes measured off in progress from not quite parallel with a Mercedes dealer's door to almost past its big window. The Fener fans didn't seem interested in the gleaming silver cars locked away behind glass – out of almost everyone's league.

'Did you see *Crash*?' said Grafton.

'No.' Many of our movie conversations start like this.

'Cronenberg directed, based on a bizarre story by J. G. Ballard. These people get an erotic thrill from car crashes, so they deliberately engineer them and have sex in the wreckage.'

'It doesn't grab me,' I said. 'You'd be so uncomfortable.'

'But there's a thematic link between the erotic and danger. Or the eroticism of danger.'

'Well, I was not in the least aroused,' I said grumpily. 'And since when does everything have to be related to a film?'

'Touché.'

Finally the rain eased and a while later we all began to steam under our bin bags. Grafton and I ripped each other's off like Chippendales' rejects and tried to wring out our shirtsleeves. A man in front shrugged. 'Weather like London,' he said, smiling. He turned out to be a Turk studying in England, back specially for the game. He'd adopted Leeds United 'because everyone hates them, I don't know why', and this made him a double Galatasaray-hater, although I sensed he was secretly proud of their recent international success, flying the flag for Turkish credibility. Fener and Gala were not big money clubs in the AC Milan sense, but you could tell they desperately wanted, no, demanded, to be taken seriously.

We read the English paper, soggy from my pocket. Pundit Michael Severn boldly reckoned that the key to tonight's game would be psychology. Whichever team was better prepared mentally would probably win. Gala was in form. Fener was at home. It was 'High Noon and the Gunfight at the OK Corral in one package'. Since there was nothing else to do, we also tried the Turkish paper, loaded as usual with pale topless girls. Coincidentally, its back page had also taken an American angle to the clash by reproducing the poster from the movie Gladiator. Much to Grafton's amusement they had pasted the two coaches' faces in place of Russell Crowe and his rival. The disregard for copyright infringement was as impressive as the image (two lugs leaping at each other with long knives) was apt.

Abruptly, two lines of police carrying visors and clubs ran down the road and fanned out along each side, young men under their black clothes just like the fans, and visibly nervous. A bus came into sight and splashed past, serious faces at the window, people surging forward, a sudden roar of derision from the street that rolled down the road like a Mexican wave. 'Galatasaray bus,' our new friend shouted over the hubbub.

'What was everybody chanting?' I asked.

'Oh, we say they are sons of beeches.' Some things, evidently, were the same the world over. He laughed. 'It is nothing. Last week our Fenerbahçe bus was stoned after the game.'

We were near enough now to hear piped music floating from inside the stadium. The top of the wall was already a solid line of distant heads waving flags. Many seemed to be jumping up and down, oblivious to the long drop over the parapet right behind them. It was five-thirty, an hour and a half before kick-off.

The Leeds fan was tapping away at his mobile. 'I tell my friends in London that Galatasaray just arrived,' he said, working the keys fast. 'They watch on satellite. On Sky. All round Europe.' Again, that touch of pride. 'How much you pay for your tickets?' We told him and he whistled. 'Too much, too much. You need Turk to help you. We pay fifteen dollar yesterday.' He turned to explain to his group and they all whistled in turn, shaking heads.

'It's all right,' said Grafton. 'We're here now.'

'Let me see your ticket,' the Leeds fan said. Deciding that we were among friends, I repressed a flicker of wariness and fumbled in my damp pockets. He took a quick look. 'Oh man,' he said, and my heart-rate shot up.

'What is it?'

'Your ticket.'

'What about it? Is it okay?' After almost three hours as a bedraggled rat in a bin bag, I was far too invested to hear that we had forgeries after all. But I was on the wrong track.

'You're at the other end. Not here. Why did you come in this line?'

'Some police told us to,' I said. General shrugging among the cluster around us.

'They don't know anything. They say the wrong thing for sure. Never listen to them.' He broke off to review the situation with his mates. 'Listen. Don't worry. Stay here. We'll explain. You come with us.'

'But what about our seats?' I said. 'If they're in the other end it won't help to go in here.'

General laughter from the group. 'Seats don't matter. This ground, see? Full. Thirty thousand. So what they do? Sell ten thousand extra tickets. Black market. Big extra money. Listen. Sit where you can find.' He corrected himself. 'And no one sit anyway.'

'You mean the club sells duplicate tickets?'

'Sure. Look at the price.' He held up my ticket and waved it alarmingly. 'What, two pound? Three dollar? Thirty thousand tickets? Not enough money. Black market sales much more. Like you. Good for club. Buy good players from Brazil.'

Suddenly we were at the front. A few words from our friend and we splashed past the first line of police, then some club officials whose job appeared to be merely to look at us. Then the frisking cops found my camera even though I'd hidden it beneath my wallet.

'No cameras.'

'America,' I said. 'Aeroplane. Specially. Fenerbahçe. Didn't know. Sorry.'

'No cameras,' my cop said again, but oddly my haiku excuse seemed to work. He shrugged and let me through. I loved Turkey just then. America has its 'can do' attitude. In England it's 'No, you're not allowed to do that and it wouldn't work anyway if you tried.' In Turkey it's 'No. Oh, go on then.'

But the next short queue, the actual turnstile letting everyone inside, was our downfall. Cajoling didn't work here and before we knew it, we were being led back to the main gate and pointed to the street heading the other way. I felt Churchillian: after so much waiting, by so many, this was not the end, not even the beginning of the end . . . we will queue in the puddles, we will queue on the pavement, but please don't make us go back out there again. The police smiled and understood not a word, pointing, this way, this way. A club official waded over to help. 'Ignore them,' he said, and hope surged again. The VIP entrance was right behind us. 'They tell you wrong. Don't go down that street over there. You must go all the way round the stadium on the other side so you do not meet Galatasaray. Go to the other side.'

Further resistance was futile. Haiku wasn't working either. With barely forty-five minutes to kick-off we scampered back past Burger King and the dog-dump canal and the skanky car park. At the end of the stadium wall, whose sections seemed to be held in place by huge slabs of Styrofoam, we found a new turnstile surrounded by a brown lake of rainwater. Fording this last trivial obstacle, we proffered our tickets, found them accepted as valid and, four and a half hours after arriving, we were in!

We shuffled along, under massive blue and yellow streamers hanging from the stadium roof, looking for our row of seats. We made it to our stairway and about ten rows up before realizing that as the final arrivals we would never get close to any seats, let alone ours. There were police on the steps, theoretically to keep people out of the aisles in case of emergency. We joined them and a few hundred fans, wedged on a couple of stairs just above the crossbar, and let the scene swallow us up.

For a few seconds I thought it was an earthquake. The entire stadium opposite, solid blue and yellow, was undulating, a sort of roiling motion like water on the verge of coming to the boil. Then I realized that everyone was jumping on the spot, the entire stadium vibrating under our feet. All the people around us seemed so tall, I now saw, because they were standing, jumping on their seats, chanting like machine-guns in unison. The place was a complete madhouse. It was frightening and brilliant. And nothing was even happening yet.

Actually, something massively important was going on: the 'buraya'. On the field, just a few yards away through a tall wire fence, Fener's players were warming up, jogging together. The crowd was busy calling out a kind of sing-song with each name in turn. Right now it was the beanpole Swede Andersson, easy to spot among his comrades. 'Andersson, Andersson, buraya!'

'What?' Grafton shrieked in my ear from the step behind.

'It means "come here",' I yelled back.

'What?' said Grafton again, but there was no need to repeat. Andersson was already coming, running towards the crowd, punching the air in front of him three times like someone throwing a skimming stone across water, and then blowing a big two-handed kiss at us as the roar swelled. Immediately after the fans to our left started up the same thing and the Swede was off to pay his respects. This went on until every player had performed and only then did they leave the field. Being a manager in Turkey must be easy, I thought, at least for home games. Fener had won every single home match this season, said the paper, partly thanks to their supporters. In their last match they'd even gone three down before surging back to win 4–3 and it was all due to 'rocket fuel' – the crowd. I had assumed this was poetic licence. A modest home advantage is well known in most sports, but Fenerbahçe seemed to have found the formula that made them almost invincible. Rocket fuel, and I was a droplet in it.

It got better (or worse) when Galatasaray ventured on to the pitch. Their turn for the humiliating protection of riot police shields, even though their tunnel had an inflatable extension that took it further from the crowd. Missiles rained down, cups and water bottles mostly, although the outraged Gala coach claimed lighters and batteries afterwards. 'This evening I was ashamed of being human,' he fumed, producing a collection of Duracells and Ever Readys.

And now came the taunting, referring to Gala by their weird Swiss nickname:

> 'Cim bom bom, cim bom bom,
> hey diddle dumpling, my son John.'

I couldn't tell what the real chant was, but it was just like a rapid-fire nursery rhyme, except in a distinctly Turkish minor key. Or like that old anti-Vietnam protest:

> 'Hey, there, LBJ,
> How many kids did you kill today?'

That was more like it.

Gheorghe Hagi, just back in the Galatasaray side after a long ban, glowered at everyone. No wonder people called him the Maradona of the Carpathians, he had that same stocky build, the low centre of gravity, and the knowledge that he could do anything he wanted with a football.

There was a brief pause of normality for the Turkish national anthem. Thirty-something thousand maniacs stopped jumping and stood eerily still, like tombstones. A giant portrait of founding father Atatürk, looking like a slightly friendlier version of Lenin, watched over us as the song played and everyone sang. It felt so serious that I tried to sing too, half a beat behind, hoping no one would notice. Whichever image of Turkey people believed in, they were proud. Those stabbed Leeds fans had allegedly been insulting a Turkish flag and it was obvious that you should never do that.

The anthem ended. The players lined up, everyone near the halfway line as if there was going to be an immediate mass brawl. The game began. And stopped again, with twelve seconds on the giant scoreboard.

The crowd was to blame, once again demonstrating its power. The rest of us had thrown our confetti when the teams ran out, but along one side they had held back until now. Down came a blizzard of streamers, covering the wing like fresh snow. It took both teams three or four minutes to clear the debris, while anti-Cim Bom Bom chants echoed around the stadium. Forget the football, clearly we were in for an evening of virtuoso cheering. Gala's two thousand – obvious in red – were just as wild, setting off mass bouncing whenever we paused.

On the field, Gala looked confident and sharp, a team that had spent the season matching wits with the likes of Milan and Madrid in the Champions League. They were all diagonals and one-touch moves, quickly crafting a half-chance and then a penalty appeal right in front of us. Our goal looked big and inviting. Fener, in contrast, were one of those old table-football machines where the players slide up and down long tramlines, locked into position. The goal at the far end looked tiny and impenetrable. But this being soccer, Fener broke out on a rare attack, bursting through, and as our man dribbled around Gala's sprawling keeper, we had an age to watch him pushed wide, controlling the ball, shaping to shoot. We all jumped and seemed to hang like bubbles in the air. The ball rolled back across the field and we had no idea from our position if it was on or off-target until it shivered the netting. Goal!

Another surprise. While there was certainly a roar of relief at this early breakthrough, given the sustained mayhem of the previous minutes, the celebration was almost a reduction in intensity. Every-one waved flags, the players made love on the grass, and then we got back to the serious business of being rocket fuel, powering Fener on to victory by sheer force of support.

I say we, but Grafton and I had been largely watchers so far. But just watching Fenerbahçe, if you're standing behind the goal, is apparently not an option. It's not enough. The man next to us handed me a paper flag to wave. I thought it suited Grafton better and slipped it to him when the donor wasn't looking. A minute later someone else gave me a yellow scarf. I got the message. It wasn't a threat of any kind, more a kind of hospitality ('eat, eat, you *must* eat'). So we joined in, raising our symbols of allegiance and hooting dismay as Andersson was blown for fouling his marker as they both jumped for a high ball, simply because he was two feet taller.

Perhaps I had no choice, but I found I badly wanted Fenerbahçe to win. For me at least, Fener was the spice bazaar, crazy taxis and a fish I watched pulled from the Bosporus, smacked on the head, plopped on a barbecue and handed to me in a bony sandwich. Gala was the Swissôtel, the IMF, and fast food that's the same the world over and no bones. Absurd, but it was how I felt at the moment. Selfish tourist romance, too, but I liked Turkey just the way it was.

We were ahead but it was panicky stuff. Typical derby fare, tackles flying, lots of writhing agony in search of yellow cards. Offside against our beanpole, twice in a minute. We bayed at the linesman while Andersson merely shrugged like a local. Soon we reached half-time clinging to our single-goal lead. Gala's players dodged more missiles entering their inflatable tunnel. Up in the stands the jumping stopped and a handful of people actually sat down, but hardly anyone went in search of prawn sandwiches or lavatories. We stood there, catching our breath, numb like disaster survivors. I turned around and Grafton, eyebrows up, just shook his head slowly.

At the start of the second half, an impressive new chant.

'Fener!' cried the far end in unison, while everyone else stood still.

'Bahçe,' went the left side.

'Aralumana,' our end shouted (or something).

'Bokya-faching!' the VIP right side finished off (slightly quieter).

'Fener!' cried the far end again . . . And so it went, for a good five minutes. Until the goal.

This time it was at our end, right under our noses: a simple low cross and Yusuf Simsek arrived first to stab the ball home, thus becoming a true wearer of the yellow and blue for having scored against the ancient foe, Istanbul lore says. We leaped and hollered. People fell off their seats. More confetti came down from the upper deck. Flags waved all around the stadium except in the quiet red pocket and the impassive black cordon of six thousand police sitting next to them. (It was interesting to see that after all the fuss about tickets, there was room to seat a small army of cops.)

The second goal seemed to finish off Gala. As the crowd resumed bouncing Fenerbahçe took control and the tension eased. Whistles cascaded down whenever the Cim Bom Bom tried to attack. They gambled and brought on their star Brazilian striker, Mario Jardel. Our own less exotic import Andersson rushed forward and, some-what typically, lumbered into the Gala goalie, who took it as an insult and squared up. Debris rained down over our heads.

Have you ever tried standing on a plastic chair, jumping up and down while waving a flag above your head? Do not try this at home. I can only imagine that Istanbul schools regularly schedule time for chair jumping. The fans are like pistons in an engine, beautifully synchronized, one taking off just as the other is landing, the next peaking as his neighbour drops down. All performed with a sense of joy, freedom bordering on religious ecstasy.

With fifteen minutes left, Galatasaray pulled a goal back and the red corner started throbbing again. 'Could get interesting,' I yelled unnecessarily at Grafton, who seemed transfixed by the spectacle. Now the whole stadium was chanting and waving continuously, even wise old Atatürk on the wall seemed to be leaning forward. Which way would Turkey go?

A better team, holding a 2–1 lead with a few minutes left, would have played keep-ball, killing the clock. But not Fenerbahçe, not in this melting pot, not tonight. They gave the ball away constantly. They were flustered. Galatasaray pressed forward at the far end and obviously it was just a matter of time before they scored again. More precisely, it all depended on whether the referee would grant them enough time to manage it.

Fener replaced Andersson with a clogger. A Gala corner kick

came swinging in and was hoofed up into the night sky. The digital clock hit ninety and disappeared.

'How much time?' I shouted at the scarf-donor next to me. 'How long?'

'Three,' someone yelled back.

'No, four,' came another cry.

The police had come down from the stands and ringed the edge of the pitch. The ones near us were women. They had their plastic shields above their heads. A Fener man went down in a heap and soaked up a whole minute while Gala players ran at the referee, tapping imaginary watches – add more time! When the referee blew for a foul people thought it was over and at once there were hundreds of blue and yellow flags careening on the grass. The police quickly formed an inner square to protect the players and swept the fans away. A Gala defender took the kick and sent the ball deep into Fener's box. Another scramble, panic, hack and hope, and then the final whistle. Fans on the field, flares, the teams racing for cover and chorus after chorus of jubilant triumphal singing. We went down to goal level and looked up at the crowd. The party was in full swing and no one was leaving to catch the first boat or beat traffic jams. This mattered too much. Then the Fenerbahçe players came out again, in white undershirts and socks rolled down, for their lap of honour. I nodded to Grafton and we slipped outside, leaving the faithful to their communion.

It was cool now and the street was just beginning to fill up. A car weaved past blaring its horn, with two girls standing through the moon-roof waving big chequered flags. Grafton was pointing at a camera crew, filming the scene. He was saying something but I couldn't hear him. It wasn't noisy out here, not yet anyway, but I was deaf from the wall of sound inside. I smiled and adjusted my proud old Fener scarf as we set off for the ferry.

Bread and Circus

One day in Paddington Station I spotted a pudgy little man wearing a stripy blue and white shirt. He was sitting forlornly on a suitcase and had a label tied to his arm that read 'please look after this footballer'. Unlikely, I know, since I live in California. But suppose I flew to London and came into town on the Heathrow Express and hey, there he was. I'd go up to him and say, 'Diego, you old coke-head! Dear, oh dear, time has not been kind to you, old son. But let's let bygones be bygones. Let's forgive if we can't forget. You look like you need help. Give me your hand — no, your left hand, Diego.' There. Now, out with my trusty scythe and whack! No more hand of God, Peter Shilton's yellow card avenged and England win the 1986 World Cup.

Well, we can dream. Actually, I wish there were more Maradonas in football. His second goal, the one where he weaved through the English team like practice cones, accelerating half the length of the pitch, more than made up for the fist. A cheat? Granted, but how many times have you seen someone feign injury or dive in the box or throw an elbow? Cheating's every Saturday. Genius is worth a detour.

His best club exploits were in tough working-class teams: Napoli and Boca Juniors. Maradona is an Argentinian national treasure, but in the bright-painted alleyways down by the old Buenos Aires docks it's not just his hand — the man *is* God. I'd seen him on TV in his own seat at the Bombonera, Boca's chocolate-box-shaped stadium, presiding bare-chested over the supremely hysterical Superclásico against the 'Millonarios' of River Plate, egging on the most berserk football supporters in the world. So no matter that the proud land of the Pampas was in meltdown — IMF defaults, bank failures, mad-as-hell crowds banging pots and pans, five presidents in a month, tear-gas, pandemonium. No matter either that Argentinian football is relentlessly violent, with rubber bullets, seventy-two arrests and one man almost dead from gunshot wounds to the chest during the last Bombonera derby and worse feared this time. If I could only pick one game, this was my pilgrimage. Nothing would keep me from going.

Except perhaps the government. The previous weekend, Boca's game against Chacarita was a running brawl in the stadium. Photographers took refuge in the centre circle and the teams came off twice. Over at River, a gang vendetta left a naked, stabbed body lying in the road. At my office, Fernando showed me the pictures in *Diario Olé* and shook his head sadly. 'It is very bad now,' he said. 'Everything crazy. Four dead this season already.' On Monday the latest government threatened to cancel not just the Super-clásico but the rest of the season. On Tuesday Argentina's president thought better of it. Much safer to have the young radicals smashing each other up over football than marching on parliament again. Besides, football was Argentina's Viagra, an overexcited spokesman added. On Wednesday, public opinion polls suggested a period of limpness might be no bad thing. On Thursday, an 'enormous police operation' was announced to prevent anyone from bringing 'objects' into the stadium. On Friday, the Interior Ministry finally confirmed that the games would kick off this weekend but this was everyone's last chance. The show would go on, but the cops would be armed and their dogs hungry.

Fernando advised getting to the ground hours early, to avoid the street battles. 'If someone asks you for money so they can get flags, best to give it,' he said. 'Otherwise they kick you. Don't take your wallet. Don't take a camera. Don't shout if there is a goal. Once I was there when my cousin Crespo scored for River and I shout. Outside they were chasing me through the grass and across the train tracks and I thought I was going to die. I got into my apartment and my heart was thump, thump and I turned on television and someone else had been killed. But you'll be fine. Just don't wear blue. Or yellow. Or white. Or red.'

★

My son George lay on the floor watching *Sesame Street* upside down. Every few seconds he wiped his runny nose on his replica Fenerbahçe shirt and sniffed. When I bent down to say goodbye he let out a three-year-old's yelp that I was blocking the screen and rolled away.

'Have fun,' Claire said, wincing while our newborn baby daughter chomped at her breast. Dairy production facility was how Claire described her current role.

'I'll try.'

'And be careful,' called my visiting mother, brandishing a large kitchen knife for effect.

'We will.'

I closed the front door, bag in hand, feeling wicked and giddy like a convict on a jailbreak, and knocked over a rubbish bin brimming with both big and tiny nappies. Claire'll be fine, I told myself. She had a vast supply of balms and ointments for traumatized nipples. There was that 'what to expect' book chock full of practical encouragement. And now she had her mother-in-law to cook meals and provide a little moral censure.

In the driveway my dad did one of his dramatic pauses and shook his head. I'd been trying to pretend that this trek was an extremely unusual early eightieth birthday present for him. 'Fly thirteen hours each way to see a scary football match I've never heard of? In a country we've been at war with and where I can't speak the lingo and all in the middle of a violent crisis? Oh that sounds marvellous, Giles.' No, the truth was that I was being selfish and irresponsible, but by agreeing to keep me company, my normally sedentary father was a fellow conspirator, helping share my guilt. And there was no point, I decided, spending the weekend berating myself. Best just relax, enjoy the adventure and hope nothing bad happened. After all, *I* hadn't devalued the peso and *I* hadn't chosen the schedule for this season's Clausura championship. So it was hardly my fault.

We settled in for the night-flight down to Buenos Aires, blowing up our neck pillows and knocking back red wine. After dinner I dipped into Paul Theroux's multi-month train ride from Boston all the way to Patagonia and felt a little less the deserter. I bet people drove him crazy telling him what an understanding wife *he* must have. Then I turned to my guidebooks and mugged up on Buenos Aires. We had the basic plan of most first-timers: eat some steak, see the sights, meet some locals, plus of course the football. 'We're going to be manure collectors for the weekend,' I smirked to my father. This was Boca Juniors' nickname. 'I wonder if the River fans sing "You're shit and you know it?"' He didn't reply and when I looked up I saw he'd fallen asleep, head back and mouth open as if ready to drink. People say that little babies look like old men and it works in reverse too. I reached across and pulled up his blanket to keep off the cool recycled air, but resisted the temptation to part him on the head.

It was impossible to sleep. Dry air, flickering TV screens, a baby howling somewhere behind us. Sometime before dawn I went to the toilets, curious which way the water would spiral out since by now we must be over Brazil and well into the southern hemisphere. But of the course the pressure just sucks it away in a huge violent whoosh. I took a glass of water that tasted like a burp and sat waiting in my chair, looking out into the dark, biting my nails.

We drove past ugly apartment blocks into Buenos Aires on the back end of a huge storm. Our old taxi kept fogging up, so the driver used one hand to steer and the other to wipe at the windscreen with a soggy towel. Through the open window rain splattered on my trousers, the only pair I'd brought. My shirt was green, green, green. 'This damn cloud is following me around the planet,' I muttered to my father.

'What?' he said.

To be fair, my mother had warned me. 'He's just like your son, actually. He'll keep stopping and looking in shop windows and you can't find him anywhere. Then he pops up again. And he won't hear half what you say. So try not to lose him.'

'These cars are a bit rundown looking,' he shouted to me as we splashed along the Avenida 9 de Julio, a road that makes the Champs Élysées seem cramped and poky. I looked nervously at our driver, a proud Boca Juniors fan, but he was preoccupied rubbing his window in synch with the wiper blades. 'It reminds me of when I got back from the war and there were no new cars at all,' he went on. It always worried me when the war cropped up. My dad as Basil Fawlty. 'I drove this very elderly, very tall Austin like something out of the Keystone Cops until, oh, it must have been 1954, when a Hillman Minx I'd ordered in 1942 finally arrived. Twelve years waiting!'

'Seems slow,' I agreed, wondering if our tickets would be waiting at the hotel.

'I drove that old Austin a hundred miles up to the Midlands with a broken leg.'

'What?' I hadn't heard this one before. 'How? And why?'

'I'd been playing rugby the weekend before I was supposed to start work for Mobil. Got tackled, I suppose, but I thought I could manage the drive anyway. Stupid, really, but there it was. I remember hopping around a lay-by off the A5, hurting like the blazes. I went straight to Birmingham General and they kept me in and put a hip to ankle cast on. Turned out to be a hairline fracture. When we did physical therapy they had all of us with broken bones lurching about playing football. There was this chap calling in his Brummie accent, "Oy, you're sposed to be me goalie", and I thought, "Blimey, I can't understand a word anyone's saying."'

'Were these the same enlightened medical professionals who said you were too scrawny after living in India and insisted you drink a pint of cream every day?'

'Maybe, I can't remember. Very good preventative medicine, a dollop of cream. Still does me a power of good.'

At our hotel the desk didn't have our tickets yet so I left a phone message with Jorgé, a well-connected friend of Fernando, who was our local source. After checking TV and finding an argumentative talk show devoted to 'Boca Sin Riquelme' – how would they cope without their star play-maker? – we set off exploring BA, yet another city described in guidebooks as 'the Paris of . . .' In this case, the south. To me, it looked more like a wetter version of Madrid, cosmopolitan and European. The English had contributed football, hence Anglo club names like Newell's Old Boys, plus the railways, back in the days when we knew how both things worked.

We walked to the Plaza de Mayo past Lloyds, Chase and Bank of Boston all hidden behind steel barricades and more than a few women and children begging with tiny accordions and Styrofoam cups. At the square a few hundred pigeons were all facing the president's digs, the Casa Rosada, as if waiting for an appearance. But with buses growling past, the fountains off and the place deserted, it was hard to imagine all the big stuff that had happened here, like 'Loyalty Day' on the 17th of October 1945, when 300,000 determined *porteños* from La Boca and the other working-class neighbourhoods forced the military to release Perón.

'Madonna waved from that balcony,' I said, pointing. 'In the movie version of the musical version of the real story.'

'Maradona?' said my father, mishearing.

'Yeah, him too actually, after he won the World Cup. We can wave back at the Bombonera tomorrow. Come on, let's get a wake-me-up.'

We sat in Café Tortoni, a vintage coffee house recommended by my guide book. We were the only customers. Dad ordered espresso and I couldn't resist a *submarino* – a glass of hot milk with a bar of chocolate melting inside. Our drinks came with plates of tiny biscuits, a jug of water, two side glasses and a silver sugar bowl, completely filling the table. I gazed around, admiring the dark wood and mirrors, and a tall ceiling with a green stained-glass dome. When I'd excavated the sludge in my glass with a long-handled spoon we strolled up to 9 Julio. There was a subway station at the corner and, after we'd finished crossing all the lanes, another different subway station on the far side. We turned around and walked all the way back, so that if anyone asked, we could say that, yes, we had traversed the world's widest road in both directions.

A few streets away, BA's Obelisco thrust into the sky, one of those pointless, pointy towers like the Washington Monument or the Seattle Space Needle. Yes, we've taken our Viagra. Three girls sat on a bench eating lunch and a man walked past them, turned back and began singing. When he bowed and left after a couple of verses, the girls leaned together, giggling, flushed with happy embarrassment.

Two blocks further we reached the Teatro Colón and went on the tour with a bunch of elderly Americans dressed in shorts and asking questions about how much everything cost. The Colón is, yawn, the biggest opera house in Latin America – although barely one twentieth the capacity of the Bombonera, I calculated. Pink marble, oil paintings, a chandelier, the big red curtain – it was all shipped out from Europe, along with truckloads of Mozart and Verdi, for Argentina's high society. I loitered by a cabinet full of old violins with broken strings, thinking that with modern opera – meaning football – the tide pours the other way. Argentina exports all its top players to Europe these days. The only Three Tenors calibre performer we'd see tomorrow was River Plate's Ariel Ortega, known to everyone as the little donkey. His head-butt of the swooning Dutch goalkeeper led more or less to Bergkamp's wonder-goal and Argentina's exit from France 98. Wagner never scripted anything better.

We sat in the president's official box and tried to imagine a packed house in gowns and tuxedos buzzing with elegant anticipation as the chandelier dimmed. Imagination was our only option because the season had been postponed. There was a new phrase in Argentina, gallows humour for every victim who'd lost his job or whose life-savings were locked in failing banks. 'I've been pesified,' they'd say, as the currency plummeted daily. And now, even the mighty Opera had fallen. Ever since the Greeks, ruling classes have known that their survival depends on providing bread and circuses for the rest of us. Telling, I thought, that when push came to shove *The Marriage of Figaro* was benched but Superclásico remained centre-stage.

Back at the hotel (still no tickets) I realized that too much red wine on the plane and a day mainlining strong coffee had brought on a throbbing headache. From past experience I knew that my only option was to lie face down in the dark, groaning softly for around four hours. I told my father that he was in charge of the evening's social programme and left him collecting brochures from

Juan, our friendly concierge. I drank three glasses of water, turned the television to *fútbol* chatter ('pasión si, violencia no') and lay on the bed. Outside, the sky went dark and something like a monsoon began. My last waking thought before conking out was that yet again, I'd forgotten to bring a raincoat.

At seven o'clock my father banged on the door. I let him in and sat on the bed, rubbing my forehead.

'It's all arranged,' he said, beaming with accomplishment.

'What is?' I wasn't all there yet.

'We're going to a tango club. They're picking us up. There's dinner. I've changed money. I've been exploring too. The concierge lent me an umbrella. There's some good leather shops.'

'Tango?' I said. 'Wait a minute. Are we supposed to dance?'

'Lord, no. I think our one's a sort of history show. I can't fathom this brochure though, even the English bit.' He waved a picture of lewd women under my nose and read out loud. 'This house. Where the passions remain. International cuisine. Where Tango as forgetfulness insists.'

'Sounds about my level tonight. When do we have to go?'

'Now-ish. Oh, and the tickets came. Jolly good ones, the concierge says.'

Suddenly I was awake and recovered, tangoing across the carpet. 'All right! Bring 'em on! Let's do it!'

Half an hour later we were installed at a table for two, eating international cuisine and sipping an Argentinian Chablis called Aberdeen Angus. On the stage, a broomstick was leaning against a honky-tonk piano, waiting for lewd dancers.

'I did actually dance a tango once,' said my father.

'You're kidding.' First driving vintage cars with broken legs, now dancing tangos. This was a new face to the man who had been just, well, there every day while I grew up, trundling off to work and coming back, harrumphing at the *Telegraph* or watching the box, grumbling about the price of petrol, fiddling with the lawnmower on Sunday. Since I no longer needed the domestic kind of dad, this previously hidden swashbuckling version was rather appealing. I leaned forward and smiled encouragingly.

'It was a dance night at St Albans Town Hall. Must be nearly sixty years ago. The orchestra started up with this tango and there was only one couple on the floor. Well, I was the idiotic type of early-twenties person who would jump in and do things he couldn't.' He was? News to me. 'We thought we better help this other couple out and off we went. Managed all right, too. When the music ended everyone was laughing and clapping and off we came and they told us it had been a special demonstration by a professional couple. Haven't done another tango since.'

'Who was we?' I asked.

'You know, it's funny. I'm getting so pea-brained I can't remember the name of the young lady.'

Memory loss, I wondered, or too many girls to count? The waiter came over to top up our Aberdeen Angus and I asked him who he fancied for the Superclásico. 'Boca, Boca, Boca,' he said and pointed emphatically at his navel, I'm not sure why. Maybe a Viagra thing.

The tango show was indeed a serious history of the dance, any smut being purely incidental. I gathered that it began as dirty-dancing with immigrants and knife-fights, then it got all fancy and regal in Paris, and ended up in 1970s trouser suits like Abba. The constant through this was sex. If all forms of dancing are allusions to romantic attraction, tango doesn't mess about. It's about mating, legs locked, crotches together, he shoots, he scores. The last time I watched an obviously saucy performance with my dad, I remember aching with embarrassment. I was ten and the erotica in question was an old James Bond film: bikinis, bedrooms, raised eyebrows and wah-wah trumpets. But now we sat companionably, fellow swashbucklers admiring a cute girl's strong legs and high heels as she arched backwards, red hair falling to the stage. The music climaxed and we all broke into applause while the waiters collected our pesos and then ushered us into the waiting minibus, back through midnight Buenos Aires. It was dark and humid and electric with anticipation.

★

Sunday breakfast was terrific, although my father was confused about the egg options. 'What does "easy over" mean?' he wanted to know, chasing crispy bacon around his plate. 'I can never remember.'

'It helps finish off the runny clear stuff,' I said.

'I don't know,' he sniffed. 'The normal English way seems to work all right.'

'By the way, I think today, if anyone asks us, we better say we're from the US.'

'Pretend we're Americans?' It didn't look as though my idea held much appeal. A waiter came over with fresh teapots. 'Goodness, this is how tea used to be served in India fifty years ago,' said my father, admiring the clutter of silverware. I realized that the more I urged him to downplay being English today, the more obviously English he would probably become. It reminded me of my son back home, who had recently discovered that special delight from doing the exact opposite of any instructions: wipe your nose, don't throw that marble, chew with your mouth closed. 'Nutrasweet. Oh dear, that doesn't sound like me at all.'

Upstairs, I called home guiltily. 'Tantrum Central,' said my wife.

'It's me. How's everyone?'

'Fine. The baby was up from three till four, then George wanted to play basketball at five. George, Daddy's calling from Argentina.'

'Considerate of them to take turns.' I laughed faintly. There was silence on the line. On the muted television in my room, Rangers were playing Celtic again. It was 1–1 with ten minutes to go.

'George says he doesn't want to talk to you. So what have you been up to?'

'What? Oh, nothing really. It keeps raining. The city's pretty quiet.' Rangers mounted a wave of attacks that ended with a shot finger-tipped away by the goalkeeper. 'Well, I'd better go,' I said. 'We're running out to find plastic coats.' A replay showed that the ball had been going inside the post.

'You've got at least half a dozen piled up here,' said Claire. 'Well, good luck, whoever it is you're supporting today.'

Our shopping trip was a fool's errand. Most places were shut and nobody had an *impermeable disponible* or knew where any were. I did get a blue and yellow Boca Juniors shirt for George. 'Is that who we're supporting?' my father asked. It certainly was. I'd been in BA less than twenty-four hours, but I'd read my guidebook, been for a walk, seen a tango show. I had it all figured out.

'This place is supposed to be a great country,' I said. 'Silver, leather, beef, the boulevards, just look around. It's splendid. But the people here have been cheated rotten. Peronists or the generals' dirty war, dropping protesters out of planes into the Río de la Plata, even Carlos Menem recently, most governments have been terrible. All that natural wealth but somehow it's been siphoned away. So you have to pull for the people and that's Boca. River, they're the *Millonarios*, the posh suburbs, the haves.'

'If you say so. It's just two football teams kicking a ball.'

'Shh,' I said. 'It's symbolism, but it's real for me.'

Over sandwiches, I checked the day's paper. It said that River hadn't won at the Bombonera since 1994. The weather would be *lluvioso*, which had something to do with a cloud symbol and a lightning bolt. Security would be provided by 1350 regular cops, 10 'combat groups', 70 horses, 70 motorbikes, 4 ambulances and 1 helicopter. 45.5 per cent of the people thought Boca would win and of these, 43.9 per cent thought it would be 1–0. That sounded right. Fernando had told me that his team, River, played fancy football but Boca was happy to win ugly. When you're the people, you take what you can get.

A thunderclap announced a new storm rolling in. We ordered coffee. 'I was thinking,' said my father, 'how easy it was flying down here. Almost ordinary.'

I shrugged. 'The red wine helped.'

'I remember flying off to Calcutta after the war to work in that car factory. Very different back then.' Here we go, I thought. Tales from the Raj. 'We took off from Heathrow in this BOAC converted bomber. A Lancaster, or maybe it was a York. Unpressurized. Flew low. Very loud. There could only have been about fifteen passengers. It was four days getting there!'

'How could it possibly take that long?' I said.

'Because we stopped in Libya the first night, some hotel right by the airfield, then we all showed up again after breakfast the next morning and flew on to somewhere in Iraq. The third night was in Pakistan.'

'What a truly bizarre-sounding route. This was BOAC, you said?'

'On the second day the pilot called us up to look out of the cockpit while we were flying over Cairo. You could see the pyramids below, one of those indelible memories.'

I refilled his cup and found him a packet of real sugar while he gazed through the window at the rain. 'Why did you emigrate and head off to India, anyway?'

'I'm not sure. I was probably bored. I think I tended to take big life-changing decisions at the drop of a hat.'

I stared at my father, surprised. I'd always thought he and I were down-the-line different. I liked, in rough chronological order: the *Beano*, football, Gala Peter chocolate, Pink Floyd, neo-Keynesianism, brown and bitter, Graham Greene, leaving town, American girls, hiking up volcanoes, sporty cars, starting new careers, making chutney, bet-the-farm investments and the Euro. Dad, well, he never showed much interest in Lord Snooty and his Pals, and political arguments over dinner and all the rest just followed. It's the oldest rebellion in the book. You create yourself through all the ways you think you're different.

'Did you like India?' I asked.

'Racing my old MG was fun,' he said. 'I went on some long treks in the Himalayas. But when I left after three years to catch the P&O steamer home, I said to myself if I never see Calcutta again, that'll be too soon.'

It was time to go. I took a long shower and put on clean underwear, a sober pair that would cause no family embarrassment in emergency wards or mortuaries. I chose a grey logo-free T-shirt. I emptied my pockets and placed my wallet, wedding ring, phone, camera and passport in the hotel safe, just like an inmate on his first day of detention. Jorgé, who got hold of our tickets, had asked his wife Maria to drive us to the stadium. 'Don't wear a watch,' she told me on the phone. 'And better no designer clothes. Boca people, well, they are heavy, you know?' As I sat waiting for her to arrive, I thought about writing my name across my torso, but it seemed defeatist. No one goes to a football match expecting to get killed. It should at least be a surprise.

At half past two we were piling into the back of Maria's car. She gestured at the man in front. 'This is my dad.'

'And this is mine,' I replied.

It didn't take long to drive into La Boca. Every few minutes Jorgé called Maria on the mobile to tell her which road to take. Soon we were parking in a muddy grass field, with small boys waving where each car should go. As we locked up, I handed Maria the cash for our tickets and she quickly stuffed the notes into her purse. 'Not here. We must be very careful, please.'

We hurried to the corner where Jorgé was waiting. He and Maria embraced and we all shook hands and smiled. Fat clouds raced overhead. Behind us the stadium was in song, the single helicopter hovering above. Jorgé led us to a line of riot police and waved a plastic badge. His company operated the magnetic tickets and turnstile systems here and over at River, which, on a day like today, meant he was one of the most important people in the city. Round a corner and we were up against the Bombonera's concrete wall with blue ticket windows. The streets converging here were lined with simple painted houses and bars, blue and yellow flags flapping in the wind, people swarming around an obstacle course of barriers and fences. Another discussion with men in helmets guarding a gate and we were frisked, then allowed through. Around the open corner of the stadium we caught a glimpse of River's hordes already inside on the upper deck, most in white, chanting and all pointing together at the other end. Fernando had explained that in Argentinian football these gangs – the *barras bravas* – ally themselves with various club directors and officials and plan their battles accordingly. Amazingly, the clubs give them money and tickets. Sometimes gang leaders show up at board meetings. When an important gang threatens the manager's family, it's usually time for him to quit.

We trotted on, past more police with dogs this time, reached our turnstile and were waved inside. Up a smelly stairwell and out we came, almost on the halfway line. The seats in front of us were mostly empty since the game didn't begin for another two hours, but both ends were already packed. The grass was lush green, the triple-decker Boca end bouncing in blue and yellow, and the sky swirling. River's fans had organized themselves to mimic their shirt, white with a perfect red sash down the middle. Jorgé nodded in approval. Things were looking good in his stadium.

I grinned at my father and he shook his head, beaming back. 'This gets the juices flowing,' I shouted.

'Crikey, yes,' said my dad.

We spread newspaper pages over our wet seats and sat there, soaking it all up. Relative to Old Trafford and the Bernabéu, I suppose, the Bombonera is a dump and one day it will be torn down. But that will be a sad day for football. The stadium seems to lean in on itself, dizzy and dramatic, like people crowding around a street brawl, peering over each other's shoulders. Just above our heads, a television camera waited on a steel gantry, swaddled in plastic bags. Behind it was an executive box and as we looked up a man leaned out and waved jovially. Someone next to me said, 'Presidente.' Since everyone was clapping, he must have meant club, not country.

The rain came down harder and we retreated underneath the upper deck's overhang. I spotted a man selling coffee from a thermos flask and felt the craving. When I returned clutching four scalding plastic cups, my father wanted sugar. 'Si, si, si,' said the thermos guy, pointing at our tiny drinks. He was right. It was hot, thick and sweet. We toasted with Maria's dad and then leaned against the wall, listening to the barrage of song while the concrete shivered faintly.

'They don't like each other so much,' Maria said and we all laughed.

'River? Boca?' her dad asked us, looking serious.

'River,' I answered quickly and loudly.

'But you said . . .' my father began.

'Mejor equipo por Argentino, por mundo!' I insisted. However mangled, it was the right answer and he toasted us back.

Since there was no reserve match to watch, no players warming up, no announcements, no piped music, I was amazed how quickly two hours passed. It was because the circus had begun already: the crowd was the show. Both ends grew ever denser, the hurled abuse louder, arms rising and chopping together. Then came the Arrival of the Drums. Suddenly a neat square hole appeared in the second deck of River's end, a flurry of drumming and a big cheer as their squad took up its central position. But Boca outdid them, a procession of chequered flags and umbrellas spreading behind their goal while the drums rolled back in the stairwells, and finally a monster flag that unfurled on top of them all, billowing as the crazies pogoed beneath it.

'Just like West Brom in the fifties?' I asked my father, but he didn't seem to hear.

'Puta! Puta!' The cry went up with more finger pointing.

'What's that?' asked my father.

'I think it means "whore",' I said.

'They say "puto",' Maria corrected. 'It's a homo, you know? Hit them, kill them, I think it is the same everywhere now. All insults, bad words.'

And bad they were. Homos! Bastards! Whores! Chickens! The helicopter circled overhead and the VIP stand opposite began to fill, except for Maradona's box, obvious on the halfway line with its *Unique Rey* banner and row of empty yellow seats. I imagined that God would presumably arrive last and that if He was held up in traffic, the teams would wait in the tunnel until all was ready. Maria broke the news to me.

'He's not coming today.'

'Why not?'

'He's in Cuba. How you say, rehabitulation of drugs? Also he is a friend of Fidel Castro.'

'Castro?' my father echoed. 'What a pair.'

'And when he lives here people make him crazy all the time. Diego! Diego! I think maybe his daughters come today.'

Oh, well. A Maradona daughter was better than nothing, but I was disappointed. We'd come all this way, you'd have thought he could have made an effort.

Below us some children were hauling an unwieldy banner around the touchline. As each section of the crowd saw it, they burst into shouts of 'Argentina! Argentina!' I thought it might be about the World Cup but I was wrong. The black letters unscrambled themselves to read *Las Malvinas todos argentinas*. Everyone stood to applaud and we joined in, smiling. My father winked at me, but left it at that.

The next banner said *No Violencia* and was carried by more children wearing the colours of River and Boca. When they'd finished their lap of honour, they laid the flag on the turf and pulled off their club tops to reveal Argentina shirts beneath. I felt a catch in my throat and wiped my eyes. It might be audience manipulation but so far, at least, it seemed to be working.

At five past five the pair of bouncy castle inflatable tunnels that the players use to get on to the pitch without being pelted were collapsed and rolled up. For a moment I thought that something terrible had happened and the game had gone the way of *The Marriage of Figaro*. Instead it turned out to be the biggest act of symbolism of the day. Moments later the two teams walked out together, just like they do in normal games all over the world, but something that never, ever happens here. Down came confetti from Boca's end, the drums pounded, at least some of the floodlights came on, a roar went up like Concorde poised on the runway, and the Buenos Aires Superclásico finally kicked off.

It wasn't, to be honest, a classic. River played some clever counter-attacking football but Boca were, as predicted by Fernando, ugly. River scored after twenty-five minutes and although Boca had clear chances to equalize, they fluffed them all, to huge groans.

'That reminds me of West Brom,' my father said. 'They had this defender who didn't seem much good and every time he made a mistake the crowd would be on his back. Bob, the chap I used to go with, had a voice like a foghorn and he used to shout out the

Albion man's name, all withering and derisive. "Oh, Rick-er-bee!" Breaking it up like that. I'm sure the poor chap was trying his best. Rick-er-bee! I can just hear it.'

Ariel Ortega was no Rickerbee. The Burrito stayed cool and took a scalpel to Boca's defence. Just before half-time, he broke up the middle, laid the ball off to the left wing, pointed where he wanted the return, flicked it across the box to a team-mate and watched the resulting shot speed inside the post. River's forwards ran into a corner and threw themselves head over heels in a slightly goofy celebration. Boca's hoards chanted all the more, no sing-when-you're-winning here, thank you, but it looked ominous.

With the rain getting worse, men came through the crowd selling plastic ponchos. I tried to buy one with a fifty peso note and only succeeded in drawing attention to myself, but then a man in front helped pass along change and I clambered into my glorified bin bag, determined for once to stay vaguely dry.

'Manchester United,' said the man, turning around. So much for not being English.

'Yes,' I said. 'The big red machine.' What about them, I wondered? Bobby Charlton, probably. It was usually Bobby, and appreciative smiles all round.

'Juan Sebastian Veron,' the man said, with obvious pride.

'Ah, yes, terrific player,' I said and my dad nodded agreement as the referee blew for half-time.

I watched the River masses singing for a few minutes, feeling slightly envious that we weren't among the local vinegar. No doubt about it, the Boca hard-core had lost its spark and we moneyed folk along the sideline *plateas* were resigned and gloomy. When I turned to my father, I was astonished to see him deep in one of those ludicrous conversations between people who can hardly understand a word the other says but don't care.

'Three children, yes,' he was saying. 'This one here, my eldest, loves his football.' I was a child again, taken to the footie by my dad. 'English? I'm afraid so. Near London. Buenos Aires? Oh, just a day. Very nice. A bit wet but we're used to that! Boca? No, not so good. Bring on Maradona, I say, except I hear he's in Cuba. Oh, very busy. We saw the opera – Colón, that's the one. Funny name. Nothing on, no. Tango, yes, yes . . .' At this rate we'd have the whole St Albans dance-hall saga before the second half began. I picked up the sodden newspaper and read a River player saying that the best way to defend against Boca was to attack. Since he'd just scored the second goal, it seemed he had a point.

Half-time stretched on. Boca came back on the field to no applause at all, not that they deserved any, then River didn't show up for another five minutes. When they finally trotted out, the most spectacular sight I have ever seen at a football match happened. The Millonarios end let loose a blizzard of ticker tape and streamers, all in white and swirling on the wind. You occasionally see puny confetti welcomes at English grounds, especially if the club has a South American player. It's as if a few friends had each ripped up their match programme. But the only way to do confetti is if everyone does confetti and everyone at River was in on the act. The entire triple-decker stand disappeared behind an avalanche. All the players stood watching, hands on hips. After a while, people began scooping up armfuls of the stuff and hauling it behind the goal, but it was still billowing to the ground for the next few minutes, smothering the goalposts and obliterating the pitch mark-ings. It was the most effective takeover of a stadium by away fans I have ever seen. Although they got rid of most of the toilet rolls, Boca's second-half attacks ploughed into a carpet of shredded paper whenever they got within twenty yards of goal.

The game continued in the same vein, Boca huffing and puffing, River content to break out occasionally. One counter-attack left a forward clear on goal and he poked the ball past Boca's on-rushing keeper. We all watched as the ball rolled goalwards, fifty thousand brains performing IQ test algebra as a sprinting Boca defender gradually caught up. It became obvious that the point of intercep-tion would be about two yards over the line, curtains for Boca, but the ball hit the post and plopped back out, safe.

'That could be it,' I said.

'What?'

'The turning point. Boca's famous for come-from-behind stuff, especially against River.'

Behind the goal certainly thought so. For the next ten minutes things got loud as Boca forced corners, camped in the penalty box, dragged shots across the face of goal, headed over, always threatening but unable to convert. The crowd sang relentlessly, nothing I recognized until one chant that sounded suspiciously like the old TV theme tune 'Hey, hey, we're the Monkees'. Surely my ears deceived me. But shortly after, our own section did a rendition of 'Karma, karma, karma, karma, karma chameleon'. Not what I'd expected at the world's most lunatic football match, but Boy George would have been proud of us. Far above River's goal, on the top deck, one fan had managed to climb up a pillar and was dancing silhouetted against the evening sky. A maniac, clearly – it would be so easy to topple off, but a heady sense of triumph was building among the visitors by now. As Boca's storm faded, the rain pelted down again. After a long, long wait, this was River's promised land.

Hola! Maria and Jorgé were waving from the steps. Five minutes to go and now or never if we wanted to get out of here. I pulled a face: I never leave early, especially when I've come to a new hemisphere to watch a game. But there was no choice, and it wasn't as if we had a nail-biter. I glanced across the field and saw that the *Unique Rey* banner was being rolled up. If Diego's daughters had given up, who was I to argue? We took a tunnel under the stadium and trotted past offices and cops gearing up for the tensest part of the afternoon. As we ran around the corner of the ground another roar went up, maybe the final whistle. We squeezed the car out of its field by dragging some loose kerbstones out of the way, then we jumped inside and Maria floored it, banging her fists on the wheel and shrieking 'Yeeeeees!' – an afternoon of repressed celebration finally released. Jorgé squashed next to me in the back, with the air of a man whose team just lost the big game but who still runs the turnstiles at both clubs. The radio was already babbling with interviews and opinions.

'We scored again!' Maria screamed.

'What?' I said. 'River?'

'Oh my, it was Rojas, the defender. He ran seventy yards, played one–two with Ortega and did a big chip over the goalkeeper. He never scores. They say it wasn't a goal, it was a *golazo*. And the River team made like a pyramid to celebrate it.'

'And we missed it,' I said. 'Damn.' The rain bucketed down.

'Oh, there's more,' said Maria. 'Boca had one man sent off in the end.' She glanced back at Jorgé, eyes sparkling. 'A perfect day,' she laughed.

The red card didn't surprise me – I'd lost count of all the yellows – but the *golazo* hurt, even if we'd see it on television all evening. I imagined Boca's fans rolling up their flags and looking sourly across the divide at River's joy. Would there be fighting, I wondered? Maria and Jorgé were talking. 'We are both very happy,' she said, reading my mind. 'There has been no trouble today. It was how things should be.'

I couldn't disagree, although a not very nice corner of me felt a mean pang. After all that worry, we needn't have. Everyone around us had been friendly. They all wore watches too. The sing-song abuse was relentless, but nobody threw anything sharp. The game had been competitive, riddled with fouls, but it was all sporting, nothing malicious. *Pasión si, violencia no.* Evidently they'd been listening.

We sped back to the centre of town and our hotel where we all kissed and hugged, Latin-style, and said goodbye. Dad and I walked into the lobby. We were tired, finished with swashbuckling and ready for a nice cup of tea. Juan, the concierge, raised his eyebrows in greeting, possibly surprised to see us again. At the symbolic level, defeat for the people, triumph for the regime, the aristocrats, the millionaires. Romantic it wasn't, but isn't that the real story, more often than not?

Over steak and eggs we read next morning's papers. The English-language newspaper's headline was 'Argentina Warns of Anarchy' but *Olé*'s cover showed River players falling to the grass celebrating the amazing *golazo* that we'd managed to miss. The Superclásico

170

was accorded thirty-one pages, with so much juicy detail that actually going to see the game seemed a pale imitation, a bit of a waste of time. I beckoned to the waiter for more toast.

Excluding player mug-shots, I counted forty-three photos, as well as bosomy images of the three prettiest *chicas* in attendance, who were awarded 'Maradonas' by the paper. A serious article offered three reasons (incomprehensible to me) why River won and awarded another Maradona to man-of-the-match Ricardo Rojas, the *golazo* boy. Every player received an individual performance review and score. Previous River Plate victories from the archives were exhumed and compared. There was a special feature on the youngest stars playing, most of whom would be off to Europe in a season or two. The drivers of each team bus explained exactly how long their journeys to the Bombonera had taken and what the mood was like onboard. Post-game interviews with both managers were reprinted and debated. Boca Juniors fans sent angry emails but said it wasn't the end yet. The visit of a Manchester United scout was duly noted. Various foreign members of the press confessed that they had come to cover the violence but instead enjoyed a passionate experience. Both club presidents had 'football is the real winner' quotes and a leader from 'La Popular' at each end described the experience of being in the heaving masses on the top deck. Random famous people got to say that they'd been in attendance too. Members of the police explained how they had kept order so successfully, just twenty arrests and no injuries, disaster averted. A double-spread provided tables for points, goals, yellow and red cards, player ratings yesterday and season average, home and away league rankings, first- and second-half league rankings, referee performance rankings, and trends in gate receipts – low yesterday due to fears of violence and the economic crisis.

But best of all was a page explaining all the songs. For Boca, it was about pride and defiance. 'Crazy chanting at the final whistle to paint over a hard blow . . . You have to pull history from your heart . . . The people bow their heads and sing . . . "Olelé, Olalá, Don't be spoiled great Papa . . . That our sons were born . . ." There the father stays, raising his baby on to his shoulder and showing him to the party in La Boca . . .'

But the *hinchas* of River wanted to turn this family upside down. 'I'm going to show you, I'm going to show you, who's the son, who's the father.' Then after 'perfectly controlled paper snakes' to start the second half, 'Boca don't go, Boca come. Stay to watch River. You're going to have fun.' And to finish, singing in the rain with drums and firecrackers all around. 'Let's all sing that Nuñez is partying down. Let's all sing that carnival's in Nuñez.'

In the taxi to the airport, there seemed no point in talking about the game. What else was left to say? Our driver stopped half-way to refuel with high-pressure gas. Petrol, he grumbled, cost twice as much. Before pumping he carefully opened both rear doors, presumably so that we could leap out in the event of a fiery explosion.

My father was bringing back a bag made, according to the woman in the shop, from the skin of the world's largest rodent. We imagined my mother making polite noises and being horrified, but in any case, off he went to find the man who would stamp the form that you could take to the desk where they could approve the rebate which – hopefully – showed up on your credit card a few months later. Five pounds is five pounds.

While I waited for him I wondered if I'll allow myself to be hauled around the planet's far corners when I'm eighty? My dad: dancing the tango, swooping over Pyramids, racing MGs, making pals at the Bombonera. A little less domestic, a bit more crazy than I knew. I'll be happy if my kids say the same about me.

At the departure gate I told the woman that we'd come to Buenos Aires just to see its big game. 'We lost,' I said, and meant it.

'Never mind,' she said, handing back our tickets with a wonder-ful smile. 'Come and see Argentina again. Better luck next year.'

'And the same to you,' I said, smiling back.

Behind Enemy Lines

'It was pretty hostile out there. I suppose it was what everyone expected from the fans, and in that respect they didn't let anyone down, did they?'

Les Ferdinand, Tottenham Hotspur

'Everyone has opinions but enough is enough now.'

Sol Campbell, Arsenal

'If the bus was ambushed, it is appalling, but it is a police matter.'

David Buchler, Vice Chairman, Tottenham Hotspur

'I suppose they're all loyal fans who love their mother.'

Police officer in riot gear

Better fess up straightaway: I support Arsenal.

So no showing up at this episode of the North London derby claiming journalistic neutrality. I'm a Gooner. Have been since 1970, when our family moved down south from the Midlands and West Brom no longer cut much ice in the school playground, bless their baggy trousers. I knew I wanted to support a big red team so I stood at the window of a sports shop looking up at the scarves and shirts. Ruling out Man U was easy enough, Liverpool were tempting – you got to sing 'ee eye addio' – but Arsenal sucked me in: the funny name, cannons on their shirt. Crucially, nobody I knew already supported them, so it would be like being the first kid to show up in boots with zips or puffing fake cigarettes loaded with talcum powder. When I discovered that my great grandfather had played for Woolwich Arsenal before running a pub in Digbeth, it felt like I'd picked a club already in me.

They repaid my faith almost at once with a jackpot, Charlie George lying famously on the Wembley grass with his arms in a big V and, while I pressed my ear to the wooden Grundig radio in our living room, a last-gasp victory in the season's last match to win the double at, let's see now . . . oh yes, Tottenham.

It's been a spirited rivalry ever since the Gunners manipulated a place in the new First Division instead of Spurs at the end of World War One. Someone picking a London derby based on symbolic divides might have gone for suave south-west Chelsea against the chirpy East Enders of West Ham. But Spurs and Arsenal get their special edge from being next door neighbours and both sides have had their moments. I shudder at the memory of the 1991 cup semi, when Gazza's long-range bomb destroyed Arsenal's bid for another double or, more tenuously, the 1995 Cup Winners' Cup Final in Paris when Real Zaragoza beat us with an absurd last-minute forty-yard lob from somebody who once played for Tottenham. This sort of ridiculous stretching for reasons to gloat only shows how in recent years we have been far more successful than them. Spurs' hungry captain Sol Campbell came to the same conclusion, swapping shirts to sign for the Arse so he could win things. After months of 'I'd love to stay here', White Hart Lane saw this as a betrayal, just like Luis Figo quitting Barcelona for Madrid. For Campbell's first return as a Gunner, Spurs fans were planning a 'Minute of Contempt' by turning their backs on him. But compared with Barça's mass whistling a year earlier, I was sceptical of such a low-key protest. How like Tottenham, I thought. All stand facing the wrong way – that'll show him. Nevertheless, things would probably be spicier than usual come Saturday afternoon.

I hate Arsenal/Tottenham games. Like most local derbies and

cup finals, the stakes are too high for anything other than a hectic slugfest. Victories, while sweet, are unbelievably enervating and defeats are too appalling to endure. Recently the games have been ending up as unsatisfactory draws, usually dominated by Arsenal (honestly, just read the papers) yet where Spurs score and we're left to claw some late saving equalizer and we lose two points on the other big red teams. But this particular game stood to be easily the worst I'd suffered through. Obviously Tottenham would win. They were at home. Saviour Glenn Hoddle, manager of the month, was at the controls. The whole Sol thing would provide them with bags of extra motivation. But the real terror was that I would be wearing a jacket and tie for the first time ever at a soccer match. According to my well-connected friend David, we were going as guests of the Chairman of Tottenham Hotspur Football Club.

We scrambled out of the house at around ten, David hurrying the big Audi through Richmond, me in the passenger seat and Zach and Joe fidgety in the back. Our day of total football was beginning at grass-roots level, with Zach's practice session.

'Do you have your boots?' David asked his eldest.

'No,' said Zach.

'Well, where are they?'

'At home.'

David turned the car around and phoned home. 'Boots,' he said.

'I was trying to remember them but I forgot,' the seven-year-old said mournfully. And then, more hopefully, 'Are we going to be late?' On the theory that many mistakes are secretly deliberate, I wondered if this might be a day that Sol Campbell would come to work without his footwear.

'Zach,' David said, gathering himself, 'we all have to remember things and it's really important that you try very, very hard to remember things too.' David ran a large and volatile technology company. When I asked him if managing hundreds of geeks made him a more effective father of young boys, he laughed. 'It's probably the other way round.'

Zach's session was already under way when we finally arrived.

Beckham was there, two Owens, and a Sheringham. Arsenal's sole representative among the replica shirts was bizarre but oddly typical: Grimandi, an uncompromising French midfielder whose elbow was occasionally found in the face of creative opponents. We left Zach in the care of an overly serious coach who kept the balls in a bag and the lads sprinting between plastic cones. One of the miniature Owens tripped and lay panting on the mud. In twenty years' time, when England are still fielding teams of hard-working chasers with limited ball skills, this is why.

David borrowed a ball and we found a spare patch of grass for a kick about with Joe, not yet old enough to be drilled. We played three and in, except Joe invented new rules to thwart every goal: no dribbling, no bounces, no passes. When all else failed he fell back on the classic ruse of gleefully moving the imaginary goalposts. 'Missed!' he shouted, as I toe-poked David's cross over a cone.

By the time we retrieved Zach my suede shoes and crisp black trousers, suitable for meeting Tottenham directors, were spattered with mud. David noticed me looking at his jeans and work boots. 'I told them you were writing a book,' he explained. 'That's why we might get a call, but it would only be you going in to see them, not me.'

'Pity I look like I've been pulled through a hedge backwards.'

'You could say you'd been brawling in the stadium.'

'I thought we were sitting in the Tottenham plutocrats section.'

'We are,' said David. 'But it's a tough gang. How do you think the camel-hair-coat brigade managed to become plutocrats in the first place?'

We crawled through dire traffic towards Hammersmith Bridge on the way to lunch at an avant-garde Greek place somewhere in North London. This was one of the things I liked best about visiting London: nobody eats English food any more. 'How was practice?' David asked.

'All right,' said Zach.

'Daddy, why do you support Tottenham?' asked Joe. Good question, I thought.

'Turn left in one hundred yards,' said the Audi.

'Daddy, is it because it's nearest Richmond?'

'I wish it was near Richmond.'

'Turn left now,' said the car.

'No chance,' said David. 'It doesn't think Hammersmith Bridge exists,' he added.

'So why *do* you support Tottenham?' I said. 'I must say I find it reassuring. Doesn't matter how sensible or successful someone gets, wonderful wife, talented kids . . . they can still be a total plonker about football. Like a character flaw or a personality foible. It's very humanizing.'

'Absolute rubbish.'

'But, Daddy, I can see Hammersmith Bridge,' said Joe.

'Make a U-turn immediately,' said the car, sounding panicky.

'When we got this car the bridge was closed because the IRA had bombed it. We need to buy some sort of update.'

'Why did the IRA bomb it?' said Joe.

'I was new at my school and I didn't have many friends. There were a couple of boys I got to know and they were Spurs fans so I started going too. It was something we shared.'

'That's funny. I chose Arsenal for the opposite reason – no one else had them.'

'Are we going to fall in?' said Joe as we reached the river.

'Does that say more about you or your team of donkeys?' David managed, as usual, not to utter Arsenal's actual name. He frowned at the navigation system map as our flashing triangle reappeared on the screen following our miraculous leap. 'There's something wrong. It's trying to take us to Hackney.' He pulled out his mobile again. 'Phil, hi, it's David. Where is this place? That's what I thought. So how d'you spell it? . . . That's the problem, then. All right, half an hour, grab us a table.'

'Are we nearly there yet?' said Joe. 'I'm hungry, Daddy.'

David turned to me. 'The system's heading for the wrong road. We need Myddleton with a 'Y'. Can you reset it? It's too fiddly while I'm driving. Just use that little wheel and pick out each letter.' I set to work and reached M-Y-D before being overcome with nausea and flopping back as we wound past Paddington.

'Daddy, shall I tell you who I support?'

'There it is,' said David, pointing at a list of roads. I hit 'select' and the Audi responded with a crisp 'recalculating route'.

'Salman Rushdie supports Tottenham,' I teased.

'And Osama Bin Laden was a Gooner.'

'Daddy?'

'Yes, Joe. Please tell me who you support.'

'Fulham.'

'Fulham? Who said you could support Fulham?'

'But it's so much nearer Richmond.'

At one-thirty somewhere in North London's scruffy mess, David called again and asked Phil to order five *mezes* so they'd be on the table when we arrived. 'Huge plates of everything,' he told the boys who were worried about not getting to choose from the pictures. Phil, it turned out, was the Head of BBC Sport and another Spurs plutocrat. This seemed typical of the BBC, some-how, although I didn't say anything. They already had Gary Lineker. Whatever happened to impartiality and fairness? Arsenal fans ought to boycott the licence fee. I said I didn't think the BBC had much sport any more, thanks to satellites and bidding wars, but David insisted that under Phil, the Beeb was planning a storm-ing comeback after years in the wilderness. Just like Tottenham, I said.

We found a parking space, crossed over and jogged down Myddleton Road, David carrying Joe while Zach held my hand. It seemed too quiet, just apartment blocks and blank brick walls. Two obviously stoned teenage girls were leaning over a balcony. They giggled when we asked if there was a place to eat nearby. David got on the phone again and reached Phil, who had heaped platters filling his table and was already well into his second kebab. 'We can't see it,' David said. 'Fifteen, I know. But it's a block of flats. Spell it again. Right . . . right . . . oh, bollocks.'

It was a classic computer error. The Audi had done exactly as we'd told it and led us to Myddleton Road. A few miles away was Myddelton Road, the BBC's Phil and five plates of *meze*. We ran back to the car, David furiously grovelling to the Head of Sport and encouraging him to eat heartily. Already the narrow streets were congealing with pre-match congestion. We were out of time.

'But what are we going to do?' asked Zach. Kebabs had been heavily marketed all morning. 'We've been in the car awfully long.'

'You have reached your destination,' said the Audi brightly, as David fired the ignition.

'Shut up,' he said, turning off the map savagely.

'I'm *so* hungry.' Joe sounded near tears.

'Doesn't your company make this sort of software or chip or whatever it is?' I asked, feeling equally hard done by.

'That's it,' David cried. 'We'll get chips in Tottenham High Road. Fish and chips all round.'

'And Smarties!' said Joe, sensing the moment.

'And Smarties,' David conceded.

White Hart Lane – like most London grounds – is cramped, hemmed in by old streets and terraced houses. I began to grind my teeth as we walked up Bill Nicholson Way (the club's manager when they won the double four decades ago) and lined up for ridiculously narrow turnstiles. Obviously fat Londoners must support Chelsea or West Ham, Tottenham was only for the thin. As David had promised we were indeed among the white collar mob, trenchcoats and tasselled loafers, accessorized with the latest Nokias. But it felt cockney all the same, street-smart lads who went to the City, coined it while the going was firm, and acquired a season to the successful blue seats of the West Lower. We sat in row three near the corner flag and unwrapped lunch, in my case a runny steak pie and a chip butty, even if I was an honorary plutocrat for the afternoon. The announcer was warning people that the club would not tolerate any racist abuse: well said, and hardly an issue all afternoon, except for a relentless tirade against the French which apparently didn't count. Now the loudspeakers were blaring out a series of knees-up Tottenham songs and I cringed as a jumbo screen at the far end showed Tottenham heroes of old sticking it to lumbering Arsenal centre-backs – goal, goal, goal.

A couple of years ago this medley would have been a welcome

blur. My vision started deteriorating at school and I accelerated the process by squinting ever harder, rather than risk humiliation by appearing in National Health specs. My bluff was called when I worked for a bank and a colleague saw me bending close to count my stacks of money, just like Scrooge. I veered between contact lenses and glasses but as I got older my vision dwindled until I was down to six inches, the top line on the chart. In desperation I went under the laser and emerged two minutes later with twenty-twenty eyesight, a medical miracle. The only negative is the acrid stink a burning eyeball gives off. (Just hold your breath.) I should have done it years ago but for the advice of two friends. One was my school bridge partner, The Grouch, who went on to become one of Britain's top laser physicists, presumably designing space-based weapons of mass destruction these days. Grouch knows his stuff. He didn't like the *Star Wars* films because, he said, real laser swords don't clank. And he didn't like the idea of a real laser beam anywhere near his precious apple pies either. Then there was David who had heard a wild story of early Russian experiments which worked perfectly for ten years until one fine day everyone's eyeballs shrivelled up like raisins. That'll be an interesting morning.

When the teams walked out, up went thousands of white balloons neatly printed with 'JUDAS', spilling on to the edge of the pitch like an abundance of spare balls. The Minute of Contempt was a bust: most fans were enjoying booing far too much to be quiet and turn away. 'You can stick Sol Campbell up your arse,' the Spurs end chorused. While Zach and Joe looked shaken at this display of wit, Campbell, who had remembered his boots, pretended not to notice and performed a series of high-fives with his new red team-mates. When the game began, almost immediately he launched a clattering tackle that knocked over two Tottenham players like skittles and the booing spiked, especially when tough-guy referee Jeff Winter made 'get up' gestures at the toppled Spurs. All around me, guys in cashmere coats leapt from their seats to spew non-racist abuse into the dimming afternoon. Loathing in the gloaming, I thought grimly.

I was feeling slightly sick – my chip butty wasn't in the same league as Barcelona's hotdogs. That and typical derby anxiety together with my precarious position as an imposter. Being forced to endure ninety minutes of anti-Arsenal rhetoric without the usual release of being able to shout back was a recipe for premature ageing.

There's a lot of singing at English games, most of it pretty mindless. But when you're an imposter, instead of joining in you sit sullenly listening to the words and it gets worse. 'Oh, Teddy Teddy . . . Teddy Teddy Teddy Teddy Sheringham.' I mean, please. As for 'Glenn Hoddle's blue and white army', it doesn't even scan properly. The only club where that chant ever had any rhythmic wit was Watford. 'Elton John's Taylor-made army,' summed up the Hornets in five words.

'Look after the boys,' David said, heading back into the stand. Arsenal promptly won a corner in front of us and Campbell's arrival in Tottenham's penalty area set off a new shower of spittle and venom.

'Does Judas play for Tottenham?' Joe wanted to know.

'Of course not, silly,' said Zach. 'He's thousands of years old.'

'Hey Joe,' I said conspiratorially, 'I think it's cool you support Fulham. There's loads of goals and it's right by your mummy and daddy's house.' And then, through gritted teeth, 'Come on you reds' but the ball wafted gently like a patted balloon into the keeper's gloves.

To be fair, Arsenal's songs are almost as bad. One–nil to the Arsenal? In fact, I realized that Arsenal and Spurs share a common vocabulary. We call them scum. They call us scum. They call us Gooners. We do too, and we call them Yids which gnawed at me until I discovered them chanting 'Yiddoes' at corner kicks. I don't think there's any Semitic issue dividing the clubs. Being in North London both have Jewish fans, but Jewishness is a definite element of Spurs' sense of self, hand in hand with supposedly playing intelligent cosmopolitan football and being a generally decent, inclusive sort of club.

Not that there was anything intelligent or decent going on today. One of the papers described the first half as 'two pit bulls fighting over a bone' and that was generous. The Tottenham dog was looking tougher and managed to hit the bar once. It even wrestled the bone into Arsenal's net near half-time but the referee saw a hand make contact. Typically, Arsenal's generous Olympians (I was delighted to see Grimandi playing) attempted to turn this let-off into a red card for Spurs' offender, but nothing doing. Into the kennels, 0–0 and a ten-minute breather for the boo-boys.

David returned with a bag of Smarties. I stared gloomily at an orange one in my palm. After fifteen years abroad, London no longer matched the older version of the software in my head. French bistros had replaced all the caffs. The Post Office Tower was called something else. Bus stops sported electronic signs that told you it was seventeen minutes until the next number nine. Phone boxes weren't necessarily red. Notting Hill was glamorous. My old expertise had been whittled away in a million daily increments until this big grey city, while still apparently London, might as well have been Addis Ababa. Since when were Smarties like horse-sized pills?

Ten minutes into the second half I began to dare to hope that my usual traumatic luck might be about to change. The previous three times I'd flown six thousand miles to watch Arsenal play they had lost in extra time (Benfica, European Cup, 1991); lost with the last kick of extra time (Real Zaragoza, Cup Winners' Cup Final, 1995); and lost on penalties following extra time (Galatasaray, UEFA Cup Final, 2000). After the Zaragoza debacle I'd visited David in London. Back then he had a rather less exalted corporate position and we spent the first five minutes spying on prostitutes picking up Johns outside his office window. Then we chatted for a while until he could restrain himself no longer and burst out 'Nayim!' – the ex-Tottenham man whose lob had beaten us. But today, years later, revenge might be at hand. The Gunners were creating diagonal patterns, the lilywhites had stopped almost scoring and even the booing was sounding like a chore. Grimandi, of all people, managed a decent shot. Some idiot lobbed a bottle at Campbell. With a bit more luck, Tottenham would be in trouble too.

I was two days shy of forty. After years wondering what all the fuss was about I now saw first-hand why it's an occasion for black balloons. Mathematically you have to assume it's half-time. Already you're either thinning on top, fattening below or both. Big life choices: made. Sperm count and brain cells: swan-diving. Family commitments requiring sensible economic behaviour: escalating. Ability to bend down without creaking: fast disappearing. No wonder nostalgia is such a big seller in the wrinkly market.

In our mid-twenties, David and I played on the left and right sides of a co-ed soccer team under the Northern Californian sun. It was a brilliant time. I drove a zippy little Italian convertible, David a bouncy American land-yacht whose wing-mirror dangled rakishly from the side by a cable. We had suntans. We had sleek Stateside girlfriends. David, in particular, had perfected the recipe for being seductively British in America: worldly eloquence delivered with an accent everybody found spellbinding, plus a dose of laddish whimsy delivered with super-soaker water guns. To seal the deal, David would let women know that he had studied Buddhist techniques of hot oil massage. Who could resist such an act? Not us actors, certainly.

By now it was dark and getting cold. Zach and Joe were huddled under their dad's coat as we approached the end of what was beginning to look like stalemate. This would be a modest step in the right direction as far as I was concerned, but hardly the birthday present I was secretly hoping for. There's no doubt that the North London derby is a great one: it's been going on for donkey's years and the two clubs find each other deeply irritating. Arsenal are boring (not true any more), lucky (not when I'm there) and successful (not enough, I want more). Tottenham's sin is the pretension of royalty: that there's a Tottenham way the game ought to be played and that their name is on the cup by divine right when the year ends in a one. But even great rivalries throw up goal-less draws.

Arsenal scored. Howitzer from thirty yards. Diving keeper, stretching fingers, bulging net and red shirts racing towards their fans in the corner. Involuntarily I was six inches out of my seat with 'Goal!' forming on my lips when a middle-aged man three rows behind beat me to it. He stood and cheered and then he danced a little jig in his camel-hair coat. He did it for me so I wouldn't have to. People turned and glared and stood up, yelling back. Quickly stewards in yellow appeared on all sides. I noticed that lines of police were already fanning out behind Arsenal's goal, taking up position for the final whistle. The plutocrats around us were morphing into werewolves, red-eyed and baying at the night sky. 'Fuck off. Fuck off out of it. Get him out of there.' But the Gooner didn't want to go, at least not quietly. He looked like he'd had a few already and now he got a few more, chucked over him by furious home fans. He laughed and shook his coat off like a wet dog. Arsenal almost scored a second and he did his dance again.

'Surely he has a right to sit there, whoever he supports?' I said to David, asking more about myself and betraying too long spent in the land of the free.

'No,' said David as the stewards closed in, grabbing my fellow infiltrator by his coat lapels and hauling him off to general cheering. 'He's inciting trouble. It's for his own safety.'

'But you support Arsenal too,' said Joe loudly. I smiled at him in horror. Shut up, you little monster. 'Do you have to leave for your own safety? Will we have to leave as well?'

'No,' said Zach, older, wiser. 'We support Tottenham Hotspur. So we're all right.'

Ninety minutes up, four to go and for the first time I could hear Arsenal's fans singing about winning away. I joined in, in my head, as our goalkeeper made a sensational save, one-handed and falling the wrong way. Suddenly I'd found my passion for the game after an hour and a half of faking neutrality. I felt the dam break and adrenalin surged through. This wasn't about birthday presents, or better luck, or sliding politely into middle age like T.S. Eliot wearing his trousers rolled up. This was simply today. The dumb, drunk, ejected Gooner had it right. He might have looked middle aged but he wasn't acting it. Life's to be celebrated, even if all you're doing is spectating. No one dies wishing they'd spent another quiet day head down at the office. 'Can't get it done against the big boys,' someone next to me was saying and I wanted to laugh out loud. Another sixty seconds, I told myself as Arsenal broke upfield, and I will. 'Go 'ome you French scum,' yelled someone else. They'd lost and they knew it. I clenched the tie in my jacket pocket. Little chance I'd be needing it now. I pictured Tottenham's directors up in their special box turning into werewolves themselves, hurling Spode china at the windows and tipping over their hors d'oeuvres cart. Jingle bells, jingle bells . . . The referee was running with his watch out, obviously watching the seconds count down. When he blew I was going to stand on my stupid blue chair, throw both hands in the air and roar like a lion encircled by hyenas and jackals. What a way to go.

The car wasn't moving. Saturday evening and the North Circular artery was clogged. The pokiest road I know in the whole of Los Angeles is called Dellwood Lane and it's wider than the bloody North Circular. We listened as the host on Five Live's call-in rendered his verdict: 'Lots of atmosphere at White Hart Lane today. It wasn't pleasant. Hope that's it finished with.' I'll say. As Arsenal's team coach left the ground a squad of tanked-up home fans – plutocrats, I'm sure – had bombarded it with bottles from the pub next door. Meanwhile David was in his own running street battle with the Audi, refusing to turn on to the M11 and take a sixty-mile detour home. I sat there steaming, wishing I had a cat to kick. Things were no better in the back where the children had cabin-fever and were rapidly descending to lower life-forms.

'So what do you really want to be doing?' David was trying to steer us to a higher plane of discourse but it wasn't working.

'This is a question about being forty, right? When's yours?'

'January. No, you idiot, I am simply not going to turn right. I'm just doing some mulling about goals for life.'

'Oh that's easy. See Arsenal hold a lead and actually win a game before I die.'

Tottenham's equalizer at the death had been devastating, the cross into a packed box, a swivelling volley, covered by our goal-keeper except that instead of him knocking down the ball, it pushed him aside and rolled into the net in a weird breakdown of normal Newtonian physics. Hundreds of Spurs players slid on their knees right into our corner, cavorting with the leaping hyenas while I sat with my hands on my head mouthing the f-word over and over. Three seconds after we kicked off, the game finished and 'Glory, Glory, Tottenham Hotspur' blared around the ground as if they'd won the league instead of merely rescuing a point at home. I was having great difficulty swallowing.

'Beyond football,' David said, as if there was such a thing.

'I don't like goals for life,' I said. At least the Tottenham directors hadn't summoned me, so we'd escaped immediately. 'I mean, I have stuff like try to get some exercise and remember to pay the gas bill, but the long term's too hazy.'

'That's precisely why goals are good.'

'All right. Drive a Ferrari round a banked turn at Monza, feeling the tyres grip and the engine howling, needle in the red.' I'd never given this a moment's thought before. We inched past a sign for Hackney.

'That's a great one.'

'Ow! Daddy, Zach pulled my willy and it hurt my finger.'

'Health, I'm starting to value that,' I carried on, trying to sound less crass and materialistic. 'Travel. Join in. Be open. Be passionate.' Christ, I sounded like a supermodel. 'The trouble is, everyone has more or less the same list. We all read the same happiness books.'

'You're a liar. He pulled my willy first.'

'Sit apart and stop it,' David shouted. 'Sorry. Which is why I think it can be helpful to perform a self-check every now and then. What am I doing? Do I enjoy what I'm doing? Am I discovering new stuff? I feel incredibly lucky that I love my work, for example.'

Presumably performing self-checks was how someone became chief executive of a cutting-edge company. Suddenly I felt tired and fed up. 'Do you still sprinkle pepper on your fruit?'

'Sometimes,' David laughed. 'Why?'

'I remember watching you peel open a packet years ago and thinking it must be another bizarre ploy to attract girls.'

Now we had music on the radio. Mick Jagger and a choir of

angelic boys were singing 'You can't always get what you want', and I looked at the glowing control panel for an off-button.

'It brings out the flavour.'

'Daddy, he did it again. He pulled my willy again.'

'Boys!' David spun around. 'If I have to stop this car I will be very angry.' Since we were travelling at barely five miles an hour, having to stop didn't seem to me like a big deal.

'But Joe started it.'

'Listen to me. I want no willy games please. If there is absolute silence for four minutes there will be a Smartie.' Absolute silence began immediately. David grinned at me. 'There's advanced management techniques for you.'

I had a boozy dinner with my family at a clubby colonial Indian near Marble Arch, all verandas, awnings and foo-foo cocktails. It was a bit of a wake really, but my mother gave me three Walnut Whips for the flight back to America. My brother Toby came from York, arriving towards the end of the meal after a manic drive down the motorway only to be roundly teased about his new girlfriend. My sister volunteered to come on future football trips if they were suitable venues for shopping and day spas. There was no surprise cake or singing, but we did all manage a roiling argument with my father about the state of the trains (heinous), mobile phones (outrageous) and world peace (hopeless). I used to think it was my job to annoy him by being radical. ('I think the government should nationalize Lincolnshire and cultivate marijuana as an export crop.') Nowadays I realize that it's his job to play the role of codger. Gets me every time. At last, I caught a late cab back to Richmond which cost more than dinner and collapsed in bed.

The Sunday papers were kind to Sol Campbell for surviving the 'ring of hate' at 'White Hot Lane', although man of the match felt more like a plot summary than a performance evaluation. David was serving up eggs on toast before the boys' rugby practice.

'More for me! One more helping. Now!'

'Me too!'

'Magic word boys. What's the magic word?'

'Abracadabra!'

I rested my chin on the lip of a coffee mug and let steam waft over me, content to watch all this chipper early morning energy. 'I see Fulham did well,' I called, when Zach and Joe sped off in search of shirts and coats.

'And boots,' David shouted as they thundered upstairs. 'So, happy birthday. The big four-oh. How do you feel?'

'Hungover. Anyway, I've still got one day to go. It's only a number, isn't it? Just because we count in three hundred and sixty-fives and everyone thinks zeros are meaningful ... but nothing real is any different.'

'Good to hear you rising above the usual defensiveness,' said David. 'But I'm so glad you called. We'd never have bothered going otherwise. And all square, honour intact.'

'Yeah, jammy Tottenham. Bottle-tossers. I was sure we had you this time. It was going to be my happy ending. What use is a draw?'

'Your lot didn't deserve it. It wouldn't have been fair if they'd sneaked a win.'

'Football's unfair. Life's unfair. Life imitates football.'

'Is that what you learned from your odyssey?'

'I'm trying not to learn anything from it. I just go.' We wandered out to the hall where my airport bags were waiting.

'All right then, which was the best derby?'

'They all have their own flavour, that's what's best. Istanbul was amazing for chanting. Italy – banners and smoke. Glasgow – venom. I know it's a cop-out, but each one's the best game on the planet if you're a local. Crazy really, it's still only three points if you win.'

'Any more coming up?'

I put on my coat. 'Probably. It's always football season some-where, although I feel like I've been mainlining the purest grade drugs. I've probably lost the ability to sit through an ordinary game if there isn't complete bedlam all around.'

'Are you still playing in LA?'

I shook my head. 'Don't have time. Or the knees these days. But my three-year-old has an amazing left foot. We use a beachball in the living room because George was breaking all our lamps. He's horribly confused though – keeps picking up the ball and shouting 'touchdown'. But I think if I started coaching tiny people soccer . . .'

Suddenly I missed my son badly. Last month every pen and fork in our house became a rocket, blasting into space. 'Daddy, do a countdown!' Before that it was construction vehicles. 'Daddy, did you see that cement truck?' When Beckham's injury time curler sent England to the World Cup he ran from the TV room to fetch help. 'Mummy, come! Daddy fell over. He went on the floor.' It was high time I went home.

'You saw Zach's game,' David was saying. 'That's going to the other extreme from intense, noisy derbies.'

'It's funny, tomorrow we've all got tickets to see a Monster Truck Demolition Derby. They squash each other, I think. Very big wheels. I'm not sure exactly, but it sounds intense and noisy.'

'You're taking George? D'you think he'll like it?'

'Oh, I don't know about him,' I said. 'But I can't wait.'